Equal Opportunities

ISSUES
(formerly Issues for the Nineties)

Volume 18

Editor

Craig Donnellan

Independence
Educational Publishers

First published by Independence
PO Box 295
Cambridge CB1 3XP
England

© Craig Donnellan 1998

British Library Cataloguing in Publication Data
Equal Opportunities – (Issues Series)
I. Donnellan, Craig II. Series
331.1'33

ISBN 1 86168 067 8

Printed in Great Britain
City Print Ltd
Milton Keynes

Typeset by
Claire Boyd

Cover
The illustration on the front cover is by
The Attic Publishing Co.

CONTENTS

Chapter One: The Workplace

Citizens first	1
Equality indicators	4
Women at a disadvantage in the labour market	5
Equal opportunities	6
'Glass ceiling' separates women from top jobs	8
Tomorrow's women	11
Wanted: a tough new law to promote women	13
The future: focused, flexible and female	15
Women and employment	16
Key facts and guidance for managers	18
Sex and shopping	20
Militant men declare war on 'social evil of feminism'	21
Discrimination against men	22
Gene wars	25
How women are faring in the US	28
Women and economic participation	28
Women directors	29
Women still lag behind in pay and job stakes	30
Army makes it easier for women to enlist	31

Chapter Two: Education

The gender divide	32
Science vs poetry: two views of a demoiselle fly	33
Girls outclassing boys	34
Non-fiction tempts boys to catch up with the girls	35
Problems that will arise when boys will be lads	36
Will the boys who can't read still end up as the men on top?	38
Confidence trick	39
WISE bus stops those misconceptions	40

Additional resources	41
Index	42
Web site information	43
Acknowledgements	44

Introduction

Equal Opportunities is the eighteenth volume in the series: **Issues**. The aim of this series is to offer up-to-date information about important issues in our world.

Equal Opportunities looks at sex discrimination both in the workplace and in education.

The information comes from a wide variety of sources and includes:
Government reports and statistics
Newspaper reports and features
Magazine articles and surveys
Literature from lobby groups
and charitable organisations.

It is hoped that, as you read about the many aspects of the issues explored in this book, you will critically evaluate the information presented. It is important that you decide whether you are being presented with facts or opinions. Does the writer give a biased or an unbiased report? If an opinion is being expressed, do you agree with the writer?

Equal Opportunities offers a useful starting-point for those who need convenient access to information about the many issues involved. However, it is only a starting-point. At the back of the book is a list of organisations which you may want to contact for further information.

*****

Citizens first

Equal rights and opportunities for women and men in the European Union

Citizens first

As a citizen of the European Union (EU), you have many rights that you may not be aware of. Did you know, for example, that, whatever the country you are working in, you enjoy a right to equal pay for equal work or work of equal value regardless of your sex? Or that you must have the same training opportunities as workers of the other sex?

The EU has published a series of guides explaining your rights so that you can make the most of the opportunities available to you. These guides also point out the conditions attached to your rights.

The scope and the diversity of these rights is so great that a brief description of them cannot hope to take in every individual situation. If you require any additional information, please do not hesitate to get in touch with one of the contact points listed at the end of this article.

As a citizen of the European Union, you have the right to work in any country of the Union (see the guide 'Working in another country of the European Union') whatever the country you are working in.

Discrimination can occur in two ways:

- *direct discrimination* occurs when men and women are treated differently, for example in terms of pay, solely on the basis of their sex. Direct discrimination also includes discrimination on the grounds of pregnancy and maternity since this is inseparably linked to gender, for example when a woman is refused a job, training or promotion just because she is pregnant;
- *indirect discrimination* occurs when men and women are treated differently because an apparently neutral provision, criterion or practice determining recruitment, pay, working conditions, dismissal, social security, etc., in practice disadvantages a substantially higher proportion of the members of one sex. Such provisions, criteria or practices are prohibited under Community law, unless it is proven that they are justified by objective reasons in no way related to any discrimination based on sex.

For instance, the linkage of certain kinds of benefit to criteria such as marital or family status, and the notion of head of household or 'breadwinner', can result in indirect discrimination. Another criterion which can result in indirect discrimination is part-time work, which is taken up mostly by women. For example, the fact of excluding part-time workers from a company's pension scheme will very likely affect a far greater number of women, and can therefore be discriminatory, unless the exclusion is justified by objective reasons unrelated to sex.

Your rights related to employment

Equal pay for equal work

If you hold the nationality of a Member State and you work in the European Union, you should receive the same pay of a worker of the opposite sex performing the same work as yours, provided that you both have the same employer. However, differences in salary can be justified if they are due to objective factors unconnected with sex, such as qualifications, experience, etc.

Work is normally thought of in terms of job titles. Some job titles are exactly the same for men and women doing the same job, whereas some have a male and female alternative. When jobs with different titles are essentially the same, their remuneration should be the same. For example an air hostess and a cabin steward, who work for the same company, are equally qualified and do the same work, should be equally paid; if one gets paid more than the other then their right to equal pay for equal work has been infringed.

The term 'pay' covers all benefits provided by the employer to you in connection with your employment. These benefits can be received under contract, statutory or collective provisions, or on a voluntary basis, and they can be in cash or in kind (for example travel facilities or housing), or in the form of shift premiums or overtime pay. The benefits also encompass future benefits such as redundancy benefits which will be received when employment has ended.

Equal pay for work of equal value

Male and female workers are also protected from discrimination which may occur when they are performing different jobs for the same employer. For this reason, Community law gives you the right to receive equal pay for work of equal value.

In concrete terms, this means that where a woman (or a man) undertakes work as demanding as that of the other gender, even though the work is different, she (or he) should receive the same pay and benefits unless there is a non-discriminatory explanation for the differential.

To determine whether the work performed by a man and a woman is of equal value, a comparison of their work is required. This involves assessing the nature of the tasks and the demands made upon the workers in carrying them out, such as skill, effort, responsibility, etc.

Only the nature of the job is relevant to this assessment. So other factors, like the fact that one works part-time and the other full-time, are not relevant, and cannot justify in themselves the wage differential.

In each Member State there is an authority with the power to decide if work has the same value as other work, after having obtained the necessary information. As each Member State has different mechanisms for resolving individual claims concerning equal pay for work of equal value, you should consult the relevant addresses at the end of this article.

The right to equal pay for equal work and work of equal value applies both to the public and private sector, whether the pay has been decided by

collective agreements, wage scales, wage agreements or individual contracts.

To illustrate the range of factors which may be involved in assessing work of equal value, consider a female secretary and a male production line worker employed in the same company, where the secretary thinks that her work is undervalued by comparison to that of her male colleague. To determine if the complaint is well founded the two jobs need to be compared, by analysing the nature and demands of the tasks undertaken. Job descriptions should be prepared and aspects of the duties involved such as skill, effort and responsibility taken into consideration, in order to determine whether the two jobs, though different, can be considered of equal value. If it is found that the female secretary does work which is equally demanding, but is paid less, the employer must justify the wage differential as being based on grounds other than discrimination on grounds of sex.

The employer might claim that the reason for the pay difference is that the secretary and the production line worker belong to two different collective bargaining groups of different unions, which have negotiated different rates of pay. However, collective agreements must respect the principle of equal pay for equal work and work of equal value. It is possible that the post of secretary is almost entirely filled by women, and the post of production line worker by men. Therefore, if the collective bargaining arrangements result in lower pay for a group composed predominantly or almost exclusively of women, this will constitute an infringement of the basic Community right to equal pay, unless the difference in pay results

from objective factors which in no way discriminate on the basis of sex.

The employer might argue, for instance, that the reason for the pay difference lies in the market rates generally paid for the jobs in question. In such a case, he has to prove that his argument is not tainted with sex discrimination but explains or justifies the whole difference.

Job classification systems

In some Member States, job classification systems are used as mechanisms to categorise jobs in order to determine the relative pay in a hierarchy of jobs.

When a job classification or evaluation system is used to determine the pay, that system must be based on criteria which do not discriminate against one sex. The system should therefore take into account criteria for which workers of either sex can show aptitude.

For instance, while the system may contain the criterion of physical strength, it should also take into account other criteria so as to avoid sex discrimination. The system should try to reach a balance between different factors present in the jobs without penalising those factors present in jobs typically held by women (e.g. manual dexterity, human relation skills or caring skills).

Whether your pay is determined by a job classification system or not, you have the right to know which criteria are used to determine pay.

To help assess whether workers of different sex are paid equally for work of equal value, the European Commission has issued a 'Code of practice on the implementation of equal pay for work of equal value for women and men'.

The Code, which is not binding, aims to provide concrete advice for employers and collective bargaining partners to ensure that the principle of equality between women and men performing work of equal value is applied to all aspects of pay. In particular it aims to eliminate sexual discrimination whenever pay structures are based on job classification and evaluation systems.

You can obtain a copy of the Code from the Commission's Representative Offices.

Equal treatment in the workplace

You have the right to enjoy equal treatment in the workplace, which means that you cannot be discriminated against on the grounds of sex.

Access to employment

Employers should not discriminate between men and women when recruiting workers. So, for instance, job advertising biased in favour of one sex is contrary to Community law.

However, there is an exception to the non-discrimination rule where the gender of the workers is an essential factor in the job. If it is objectively proven that only workers of one sex can perform all the tasks related to the job, then the employer is allowed to recruit only men or only women for that job.

For example, in professions such as fashion models or actors/actresses, gender may be considered as a determining factor.

Vocational training

Men and women doing the same job have the right to receive the same training and educational opportunities.

Promotion

Employers should not discriminate when deciding which employees to promote. They must consider workers in terms of aspects such as their skills, education, performance and seniority, and not in terms of gender.

Working conditions

Employers are not allowed to apply different working conditions to men and women doing the same job, notably with respect to the grounds for dismissal, but also in terms of matters such as dress code, job flexibility, etc. Your right to equal working conditions applies irrespective of whether the conditions are laid down in collective agreements, individual contracts or the rules governing independent professions.

Positive action

Community law allows EU countries to undertake several positive action initiatives. Positive action initiatives can be undertaken both by the Member State or by companies.

While there is no official definition of positive action as such, it does include all measures which are designed to counter the effects of past disadvantages, to counter the effects of existing discrimination and to promote equality of opportunity between men and women in the field of employment. Positive action can take different forms.

A first type consists of measures which aim to eliminate the causes of the underemployment and reduced career opportunities for either sex, by intervening, in particular, when career choices are made and in vocational training.

A second type of positive action includes measures trying to achieve a better balance between family and work responsibilities and the more even distribution of these between the two sexes. Examples include the development of childcare infrastructures or the introduction of career breaks.

A third type is based on the idea that positive action should make up for past disadvantages. As a consequence, preferential treatment can be prescribed in favour of certain categories of persons.

In the context of those initiatives, one sex may be treated differently from the other, but since their aim is to promote equality, such initiatives can be considered to be compatible with the principle of equal treatment between men and women.

Useful addresses

European Commission: 8 Storey's Gate, London SW1P 3AT. Tel: 0171 973 1992. Fax: 0171 973 1900.

European Parliament Office: 2 Queen Anne's Gate, London SW1H 9AA. Tel: 0171 227 4302. Fax: 0171 227 4302.

European Ombudsman: 1, avenue du Prés, R. Schuman, BP 403, F-67001 Strasbourg, Cedex. Tel: (+33) 388 17 40 01. Fax: (+33) 388 17 90 62.

© Office for Official Publications of the European Communities

Women as a proportion of occupational groups in the European Union, 1995 %

Throughout the EU there tend to be more women than men in clerical and service-related jobs

Country		Managers	Clerical workers	Service workers	Craft-related workers
Belgium		31	58	65	11
Denmark		19	73	77	4
Germany		26	67	74	9
Greece		22	55	50	15
Spain		32	53	53	8
France		36	77	73	8
Ireland		27	70	56	19
Italy		19	50	46	15
Luxembourg		25	52	60	4
Netherlands		22	66	68	6
Austria		n/a	n/a	n/a	n/a
Portugal		30	59	60	27
Finland		n/a	n/a	n/a	n/a
Sweden		n/a	n/a	n/a	n/a
UK		34	74	71	10
EU12		30	66	65	11

Source: European Commission DGV (1997)

Equality indicators

Information from the Equal Opportunities Commission

- In England and Wales, 49 per cent of girls and 40 per cent of boys aged 16 gained five or more GCSEs at grades A*-C.[1]
- In Scotland, 60 per cent of girls and 49 per cent of boys gained five or more passes at grades 1-3 of SCE Standard Grade, or one or more SCE Higher Grade passes, by the time they left school.[2]
- In England and Wales, 24 per cent of girls and 21 per cent of boys gained one or more GCE A/AS-levels at school by age 19. In England, a further 14 per cent of girls and 10 per cent of boys gained GCE A/AS-levels through Further Education.[1]
- In Scotland, 49 per cent of girls and 38 per cent of boys gained one or more SCE Higher Grade passes by the time they left school.[2]
- Of those in employment, 34 per cent of women and 47 per cent of men were qualified to at least NVQ/SVQ level 3 or equivalent (e.g. two GCE 'A' levels or three SCE Highers).[3]
- 67 per cent of women and 77 per cent of men of working age were employed.[4]
- 51 per cent of employed women were in occupational groups in which at least 60 per cent of workers were women. These groups were: clerical and secretarial; personal and protective services; and sales occupations.[4]
- 65 per cent of employed men were in occupational groups in which at least 60 per cent of workers were men. These groups were: managers and administrators; professional occupations; craft and related occupations; and plant and machine operatives.[4]
- 45 per cent of women employees and eight per cent of men employees work part-time.[4]
- Women employees working full-

EQUAL OPPORTUNITIES COMMISSION

time earn on average only 80 per cent of the average hourly earnings of men full-time employees. There is a gender pay gap of 20 per cent.[5]

- The average personal income of women aged 65 and over is only 58 per cent of the average personal income of men aged 65 and over. There is a gender gap in post-retirement income of 42 per cent.[6]
- For every 9 children aged under 8 there was only one place in a day nursery or centre, with a registered childminder, or in an out of school scheme.[7]

Sources:
1 GCSE and GCE A/AS examination results 1995/96, England, Department for Education and Employment, Welsh Office.
2 Scottish School leavers and their Qualifications 1985-86 to 1995-96, Statistical Bulletin Edn/E2/1997/6, The Scottish Office.
3 Training Statistics 1996, Department for Education and Employment.
4 Labour Force Survey, Spring 1996, Office for National Statistics.
5 New Earnings Survey 1996, Office for National Statistics.
6 Family Expenditure Survey 1994/5, Office for National Statistics.
7 Department of Health; The Scottish Office; Welsh Office

Women's earnings as a percentage of men's earnings[1]: by industry

One way of illustrating differences between the pay of men and women is to present women's earnings as a proportion of men's earnings as illustrated below. Analysing the *New Earnings Survey* data for seven major industry groups shows that in April 1997 women's earnings ranged from 72 per cent of men's earnings in manufacturing to 90 per cent in the transport and storage industries.

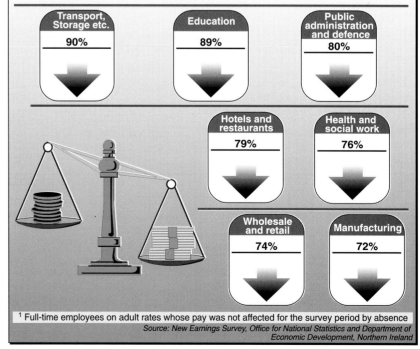

[1] Full-time employees on adult rates whose pay was not affected for the survey period by absence

Source: New Earnings Survey, Office for National Statistics and Department of Economic Development, Northern Ireland

Women at a disadvantage in the labour market

Women's skills under-valued and under-used in the workplace

Girls may be beating boys in the classroom but the paths women take after compulsory education are leaving them at a disadvantage in the labour market.

A new report by the independent Policy Studies Institute shows that the allocation of training is itself exacerbating gender inequality in the workplace and that women's skills are not being fully appreciated or utilised by employers.

Half our future: women, skill development and training, edited by Hilary Metcalf, asks why women still occupy lower-level jobs despite their much greater participation in the labour market.

Women now represent 48 per cent of employees in Britain and will soon form the majority of the workforce, and yet they earn less than men, are less likely to be managers than men and are concentrated in a small number of occupations – mostly secretarial and clerical, personal and caring services and sales.

Among the key findings

- women are less likely than men to get a degree or to get vocational qualifications. Women in professional jobs are 20 per cent less likely to have a professional qualification than men with identical personal and employment characteristics – and most hold qualifications in a narrow range of occupations, such as nursing and teaching.
- women are more likely to acquire the skills necessary to do their job from experience rather than via formal qualifications. However, these skills often go unrecognised – and unused – by employers.
- the kind of training women receive is less likely to help them

progress in the labour market and does nothing to address gender inequality in the workplace. Women's training is more often at an induction level, associated with starting a new job.

- part-timers are much less likely to get training, however. As nearly half (45 per cent) of women work part-time and many more will do so at some point in their careers, this leaves them at a considerable disadvantage compared to men. The authors found no evidence of direct gender discrimination in the allocation of training by employers. However, evidence did suggest discrimination against black women.
- family commitments reduce the likelihood of women training – but it was not just childcare responsibilities that reduced participation in training: women were also diverted from training by having a husband or partner.

The effect was less severe if the training was supported by an employer and the authors conclude that more employer support for women to train and greater sharing of housework are necessary for women to develop their skills and play a full role in the workforce

- women are more likely to fund their own training: this shows a very high commitment to employment, particularly given their worse position in the labour market. However, women need to gain confidence in the skills they do have. The authors found that women, especially the unqualified, are more likely than men to under-rate their skills.
- despite all this, women are more likely to be satisfied in their job and men were more satisfied when they worked with women.

'Despite women's high presence in the workforce, the existing patterns of training and skill development exacerbate gender inequality rather than remedy it,' said Hilary Metcalf. 'This is particularly true for women with family responsibilities, women working part-time and the least skilled women. All of this is compounded by the lesser appreciation by employers of skills most often held by women and the lesser accreditation of skills for women.'

The authors call for policies which ensure the full participation of part-time workers in training and give them full access to opportunities for promotion.

- *Half Our Future* is available from Grantham Books on 01476 541080, priced £14.95.

© Policy Studies Institute
April, 1998

Equal opportunities

A guide for employers

Introduction

1. The Equal Pay Act 1970
The Sex Discrimination Act 1975
The Sex Discrimination Act 1986

All three Acts are written in terms of discrimination against women. However men have equivalent rights under all three Acts. All have direct effect on employment decisions in relation to equality of opportunity for men and women.

The main purpose of this article is to outline the Sex Discrimination Act 1975 as amended by the Sex Discrimination Act 1986 (the Sex Discrimination Acts), as they affect employees.

The Equal Opportunities Commission

2. The Sex Discrimination Act 1975 established the Equal Opportunities Commission which has the following duties:

* to eliminate sex and marriage discrimination.
* to promote equal opportunities between the sexes.
* to monitor both the Sex Discrimination Act and the Equal Pay Act.

The Equal Pay Act 1970 (as amended 1983)

3. An employee is entitled to equal pay (and other contractual terms and conditions) with an employee of the opposite sex if:

i) they are doing work which is the same or broadly similar, or
ii) they are doing work which has been rated as equivalent by an analytical job evaluation scheme, or
iii) (from January 1st 1984) they are doing work of equal value in terms of the demands made on the worker (whether or not there has been a job evaluation scheme).

However, this does not apply if the employer can prove that there is a 'material difference' between the

EQUAL OPPORTUNITIES COMMISSION

woman's case and the man's, or (in the case of (iii) above), some other 'material factor' (provided this is in no way connected, directly or indirectly, with the difference in sex), which justifies the difference in pay. Such differences may, for example, be reflected in a London Weighting allowance or a long service payment.

A guide to the Equal Pay Act is available from your local Jobcentre, Employment Office, Unemployment Benefit Office or the Equal Opportunities Commission. A guidance booklet and a leaflet on the 'equal value' amendment to the Equal Pay Act are available from the Equal Opportunities Commission. These should be consulted for detailed guidance on the provisions of this Act.

The Equal Pay Act is to be found in Schedule 1 to the Sex Discrimination Act 1975. The 'equal value' amendment is to be found in the Equal Pay (Amendment) Regulations 1983, Statutory Instrument 1983 No. 1794.

The Sex Discrimination Acts 1975 and 1986

4. Under these Acts, sex discrimination is unlawful in the following areas:

* employment and training,
* education,
* the provision of goods, facilities and services to members of the public.

In employment, it is also unlawful to discriminate against a person because that person is married.

Advertisements which indicate unlawful discrimination in these areas are themselves unlawful.

What 'discrimination' means

4.1 Direct Sex Discrimination
This occurs when one person is treated less favourably, on the ground of their sex, than a person of the other sex is or would be treated in similar circumstances.

4.2 Indirect Sex Discrimination
This occurs when a requirement or condition is applied to men and women equally but has the effect, in practice, of disadvantaging a considerably higher proportion of one sex than the other. Such a requirement will be lawful only if it can be objectively justified according to job-related criteria.

For example, if you demand technical qualifications which few women possess, and which are not necessary for the job, this would constitute indirect sex discrimination against a woman who did not possess those qualifications.

4.3 Direct Marriage Discrimination
This occurs when a married person is treated less favourably, because he/she is married, than a single person of the same sex is or would be treated in similar circumstances.

4.4 Indirect Marriage Discrimination
This occurs when a requirement or condition, which cannot be justified on grounds other than marital status, is applied equally to married and single persons (of either sex) but has the effect in practice of disadvantaging a considerably higher proportion of married than single people (of the same sex). For example, if an employer required a job applicant to be able to work unsocial hours when in practice this would never be required, this could constitute indirect marriage discrimination against a married person who was disqualified as a consequence.

Note: Marriage discrimination is only unlawful in employment matters.

4.5 Victimisation

Victimisation occurs when an employer treats an employee (of either sex) less favourably than other employees are or would be treated, on the grounds that the employee has done (or intends to do or is suspected of having done or intending to do) any of the following:

- brought proceedings against the employer (or any other person) under the Sex Discrimination Acts or the Equal Pay Act, or
- helped another person to do so by giving evidence or information, or
- done anything else under the Sex Discrimination Acts or the Equal Pay Act such as giving evidence for the Equal Opportunities Commission during one of its formal investigations, or helping another person to present a case at an Industrial Tribunal, or
- alleged that the employer (or anybody else) has contravened the Sex Discrimination Acts or the Equal Pay Act.

However, the victimisation provisions do not apply if the allegation of discrimination is false and was not made in good faith.

How the Sex Discrimination Acts apply in Employment

5. The Sex Discrimination Acts make it unlawful to discriminate (in any of the ways defined in paragraphs 4.1 – 4.5):

- in the arrangements made for deciding who is offered a job, e.g. advertising or interviews
- in the terms on which the job is offered
- in deciding who is offered the job
- in the provision of opportunities for promotion, transfer or training
- in the benefits, facilities or services an employer grants to employees
- in dismissals, or other unfavourable treatment of employees including sexual harassment.

Exceptions

6. There are some areas where the Sex Discrimination Acts do not apply:

6.1 Work Outside Great Britain

The Sex Discrimination Acts do not apply to employees whose work is done wholly or mainly outside Great Britain. But if the work is on a British ship, aircraft or hovercraft, the Acts do apply – unless the work is done totally outside Great Britain, e.g. the Acts do not apply to employees working on a British ship where the work is entirely outside the territorial waters of Great Britain. Great Britain is England, Wales, Scotland and adjacent territorial waters. The Isle of Man, Channel Islands and Northern Ireland are not parts of Great Britain.

There are special provisions in relation to employment in the offshore oil and gas industries in connection with which the reference to Great Britain includes certain areas of the Continental Shelf, and certain parts of the Norwegian Sector of the Continental Shelf within the Frigg Gas Field.

6.2 Genuine Occupational Qualifications

In certain limited circumstances sex may be a 'Genuine Occupational Qualification' (GOQ) for a job. A GOQ can only apply to the filling of a job (by recruitment, promotion or transfer) or training for a job. A GOQ cannot be used to justify a dismissal. Also a GOQ cannot be claimed simply because the job calls for physical strength or stamina. The circumstances in which a GOQ may apply are:

- a man or a woman is needed because of physical appearance, e.g. for a job as a model – or to be authentic, e.g. as an actor playing a certain role.
- a man or a woman is required to preserve decency or privacy, e.g. lavatory attendant.
- the job is likely to involve the holder of the job doing his work, or living, in a private home and needs to be held by a man because objection might reasonably be taken to allowing to a woman –

i) the degree of physical or social contact with a person living in the home, or
ii) the knowledge of intimate details of such a person's life, which is likely, because of the nature or circumstances of the job or of the home, to be allowed to, or available to, the holder of the job.

- the employee would have to 'live in' because of the nature and location of the establishment and there are no separate sleeping or toilet arrangements for men and women. In this case the employer must prove that 'living in' is necessary and that it would be unreasonable to expect the provision of separate facilities.

- the job is in a single-sex establishment (or single-sex part of an establishment), which provides special care, supervision or attention, e.g. jobs in a women's refuge or single-sex psychiatric unit in a mixed hospital.
- the employee provides people with personal services promoting their welfare or education – which can be provided most effectively by a person of the same sex, e.g. counselling.
- part of the job is, or is likely to be, in a country whose laws and customs prevent women from doing the job effectively.
- the job is one of two to be held by a married couple.

Note: Where only part of the job is covered by a GOQ, the GOQ will apply to the whole of that job unless the employer has enough men who could do that part of the job which must be done by a man, e.g. a woman could work as a sales assistant in a men's outfitters if there were enough male employees to assist with fitting.

It is important to remember that each time such a job falls vacant, it is necessary to determine whether or not the GOQ still applies.

6.3 Pregnancy, Childbirth, Retirement or Death

It is not unlawful to give different treatment to men and women in the following circumstances:
- by giving special treatment to women in respect of pregnancy and childbirth, e.g. maternity leave.
- in the provision you make about retirement or death, except that it is unlawful to discriminate against a woman as regards age of retirement, either when offering her employment, as regards terms relating to access to promotion, transfer, training or provision for dismissal or demotion; or when she is in employment as regards affording her access to opportunities for promotion, transfer or training or in refusing or deliberately omitting to afford

her access to these opportunities or in the provision of redundancy pay.

Note: On entry to Occupational Pension Schemes

Occupational Pension Schemes must be open to both men and women on terms which are the same (subject to the modifications set out in the Occupational Pension Schemes (Equal Access to Membership) Regulations 1976) as to the age and length of service needed for becoming a member and as to whether membership is voluntary or obligatory.

6.4 Other Exceptions and Special Cases

The Armed Forces have now been brought within the scope of the legislation except in relation to acts done for the purpose of ensuring combat effectiveness. There are special provisions for the police, prison officers, ministers of religion and for competitive sports.

'Glass ceiling' separates women from top jobs

Women's progress in workforce improving world-wide, but occupational segregation still rife

Despite rapidly increasing rates of female education and participation in the workforce world-wide, most women continue to suffer from occupational segregation in the workplace and rarely break through the so-called 'glass ceiling' separating them from top-level management and professional positions, according to a new ILO report entitled *Breaking Through the Glass Ceiling: Women in Management.*

'Glass ceiling' is a term coined in the 1970s in the United States to describe the invisible artificial barriers, created by attitudinal and organisational prejudices, which bar women from top executive jobs.

The report says while women have made substantial progress in closing the gender gap in managerial and professional jobs, most female managers world-wide are still barred from the top levels of organisations, whether in the private or public sector or in political life. They hold a mere 2-3 per cent of top jobs in corporations. And even when they manage to rise to the top, female executives nearly always earn less than men.

In spite of the overall progress of women in middle management, the author of the report, ILO labour expert Ms Linda Wirth, concludes that 'almost universally, women have failed to reach leading positions in

major corporations and private sector organisations, irrespective of their abilities'.

The report cites ILO research that has found that approximately half of all the world's workers are in sex-stereotyped occupations wherein males or females predominate to such an extent – representing at least 80 per cent of all the workers – that the occupations themselves can be considered as 'male' or 'female'. And management is typically viewed as a male occupation.

In the US, for example, where women workers are equally qualified vis-à-vis male workers, they now constitute 46 per cent of the managerial workforce. In Canada, women account for 42 per cent of all managers. However a 1996 survey of Fortune 500 companies showed that women held only 2.4 per cent of the highest management jobs and accounted for a tiny 1.9 per cent of the highest-paid officers and directors. Median weekly earnings of women managers in the US in 1995 was only 68 per cent of their male counterparts.

In Japan, the percentage of women directors of companies (including small- and medium-sized enterprises) increased from 9 to 13 per cent since 1970. A government survey reported that women's share in professional and technological occupations grew from almost 31 per cent in 1950 to 42 per cent in 1990. However, the percentage of women holding positions as top managers of major corporations increased from only 1 to 2 per cent during that period.

A survey in Brazil in 1991 revealed that only 3 per cent of top executives were women and in the 40 largest state-owned companies the figure was less than 1 per cent. Another survey in Brazil found that female managers often earned only half the salary of male managers.

In Europe, the pattern is much the same. A 1996 survey of 300 enterprises in the UK found that 3 per cent of board members were women. Another survey of the FTSE 100 companies found that women accounted for only 4 per cent of directors and 2 per cent of executive directorships. Women managers earned only 71 per cent of male manager's weekly salaries. However, the earnings of women professionals in the UK reached 83 per cent of those of men, making UK women professionals one of the least disadvantaged groups in terms of the wage gap.

In Germany in 1995, a survey of the 70,000 largest companies showed that women held between 1 and 3 per cent of the top executive and board positions while their share of senior and middle management was 6 and 12 per cent, respectively.

In France, the proportion of women as executives of large companies is comparatively high at 13 per cent in 1990, but that is down

While women have made substantial progress in closing the gender gap, most female managers worldwide are still barred from the top levels of organizations

from 15 per cent in 1982. Similar reductions occurred in women's share as executives in small- and medium-sized enterprises. There was only a slight improvement in women's share of senior management posts in the financial, administrative and commercial services of large companies, from 4 to 6 per cent.

Some countries have seen progress for high-level professional women in recent years. In the Netherlands, for example, women increased their participation in senior management from 10 per cent in the 1970s to 18 per cent in 1990. In Canada, during roughly the same period, women's presence in senior positions shot up from a lowly 4 per cent to approximately 21 per cent. In Australia and Finland, women's share of senior management jobs is around 11 per cent and increasing.

In Mexico, women's share of public and private sector managerial positions rose from a relatively high 16 per cent in 1980 to 19 per cent by 1990. In Hungary, women increased their share as enterprise or organisation managers from 16 to 25 per cent between 1980 and 1990.

Even so, the proportion of professional and managerial women is higher in some developing countries such as Colombia, the Philippines, Uruguay and Venezuela than in many industrialised countries, the report says.

In Thailand, the proportion of women managers in 1990 totalled 19 per cent, compared to 8 per cent in 1974. In Singapore, that proportion increased from 22 per cent in 1992 to 27 per cent in 1996. In Colombia, it grew from 14 per cent

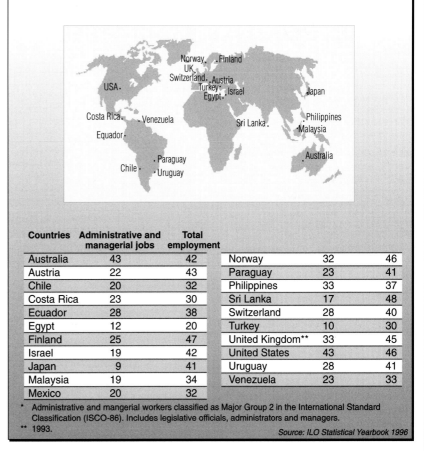

Administrative and managerial jobs

Women's share of administrative and managerial jobs* and share in total employment, 1994-95

Countries	Administrative and managerial jobs	Total employment	Countries	Administrative and managerial jobs	Total employment
Australia	43	42	Norway	32	46
Austria	22	43	Paraguay	23	41
Chile	20	32	Philippines	33	37
Costa Rica	23	30	Sri Lanka	17	48
Ecuador	28	38	Switzerland	28	40
Egypt	12	20	Turkey	10	30
Finland	25	47	United Kingdom**	33	45
Israel	19	42	United States	43	46
Japan	9	41	Uruguay	28	41
Malaysia	19	34	Venezuela	23	33
Mexico	20	32			

* Administrative and mangerial workers classified as Major Group 2 in the International Standard Classification (ISCO-86). Includes legislative officials, administrators and managers.
** 1993.

Source: ILO Statistical Yearbook 1996

in 1980, to 27 per cent in 1990, and 37 per cent in 1996. In Chile, it grew from 20 per cent in 1980 to 27 per cent in 1995 and 8 per cent of directors and high-level executives in Chile are women.

Even though the proportion of women in management has doubled or even tripled in certain developing countries, the numbers remain generally low. In 1970, for example, women accounted for 3 per cent of managers in Tunisia, which increased to 9 per cent by 1990. In Niger, the percentage of women managers and administrators rose from 3 per cent in 1986 to 8 per cent in 1991. Similarly, in Turkey women held 10 per cent of these jobs in 1995, up from 5 per cent in 1988; in Malaysia, women's share rose to 10 per cent in 1995, up from 3 per cent in 1986.

In some countries, little change has occurred in women's share of management. Women made up 5 per cent of administrative and managerial jobs in Bahrain in 1987 and this had increased by only one percentage point by 1994. The proportion of women in such jobs in Pakistan grew only from 3 to 4 per cent between 1989 and 1994. In Argentina, only 5 per cent of managerial jobs in industrial enterprises and 6 per cent in services and construction were held by women in 1995.

Occupational segregation by gender

Linda Wirth says that even where progress has been greatest, 'women generally fare best in industries employing large numbers of women, such as health and community services and the hotel and catering industry'. She argues that 'the gender gap at the top is simply the most glaring example of employment segregation by sex that prevails across the entire spectrum of labour market opportunities'.

Women in management tend to be clustered in certain activities, to the point where certain company functions are almost feminised. In the US, the increase of women's share of personnel and labour relations managers was higher than in other areas, from 21 per cent in 1970 to 58 per cent in 1991. In France the percentage of women personnel managers increased from 25 per cent in 1982 to 38 per cent in 1990. In Finland, the proportion of personnel managers who were women shot up from 17 per cent in 1970 to 70 per cent in 1990.

In the organisational structures of corporations, career paths in human resource management and administration are less likely to lead directly to the top than other strategic areas such as product development or corporate finance.

The ILO research shows that gender inequality in education and training, reinforced by social attitudes, contributes to this occupational segregation, channelling men and women into different trades, professions and jobs from an early age. It also indicates that for non-agricultural occupations, there are over seven times as many male-dominated occupations as female-dominated ones.

So segregated are certain jobs that, for example, in both Japan and the US in 1991, nearly one-half of women employed in the category of professional and technical jobs worked in only two occupations – nursing and teaching. In India and Hong Kong, more than 80 per cent of women professional and technical workers were either nurses or teachers.

In Canada, where the proportion of women working nearly doubled in recent decades to reach 60 per cent in 1991, women remain concentrated in a narrow range of occupations. In the mid-1980s, for example, nearly one-third of all employed women worked in clerical jobs, whereas only 12 per cent of men were concentrated in any single major occupational category.

A study of 27 occupational categories in the Republic of Korea in 1992 showed that women represented 70 per cent of the workforce in four categories: subsistence agriculture, health care, clerical work and food processing. In other categories they represented less than 5 per cent, including legislators and senior officials (none), corporate managers (2 per cent) and mathematicians and engineering professionals (4 per cent).

Even in countries with strong track records of government support for gender equality the pattern of occupational segregation prevails. In Finland, for example, only 20 per cent of women work in occupations that show a balanced male/female employment ratio (i.e. where 40-60 per cent of employees are of the same sex) and these jobs represent only 7 per cent of all occupations.

• The above is an extract from the report *Breaking Through the Glass Ceiling: Women in Management*, produced by the International Labour Office (ILO). See page 41 for address details.

© International Labour Office

Tomorrow's women

By Helen Wilkinson and Melanie Howard with Sarah Gregory, Helen Hayes and Rowena Young

Summary

This century has brought more profound changes to women's lives than any previous period in human history. Women make up a majority of the electorate and will soon make up a majority of the workforce, even though most of our institutions, from Parliament to big employers, have yet to adapt to this new reality.

If current trends continue, women in 2010 will be: more numerous (there are already 1.2 million more women than men in Britain); older (by 2030 a quarter of women will be over 54); more independent (a fifth of women born in the 60s are predicted to remain childless); more likely to be living alone (a third of all households will be single by 2010); more likely to be divorced (40 per cent of marriages are predicted to end in divorce); more likely to be in management or the professions (52 per cent of new solicitors and 32 per cent of managers and administrators are women); more dependent on technologies ranging from intelligent tags to mobile phones; more androgynous (31 per cent of women are now at ease with flexible gender roles); more likely to be from an ethnic minority (up from 6 per cent to 9 per cent); and better educated, with a third of each new age cohort going through university.

However, a linear extrapolation of current trends can be misleading. As we show, the interaction of the many different forces shaping women's lives could block their long march to equality; gaps in pay and opportunities could widen once again; the frustration experienced by many less skilled women could explode; and a return of traditional values could push women back into the home.

To provide insights into the likely shape of women's lives in 2010,
this report draws on two major new surveys of women's values – by AGB Taylor Nelson and Synergy – that have involved interviews with a representative sample of over 3000 women from across Britain, on Demos, and the Future Foundation's own studies of changing demography, labour markets, technology and values, and on the Henley Centre's Planning for Social Change programme. This summary sets out some of the key findings.

Society is becoming more feminine

As male jobs disappear, women's importance in society is set to rise, as is their confidence. Forty per cent of women believe that women are naturally superior to men. Women will soon make up a majority of the workforce and Britain is becoming increasingly shaped by feminine values. Values such as empathy and care, community and environmentalism, are now central to British society. Older values associated with authority, the military, and the traditional family have been displaced. Work has become more important for women, and nearly all groups of women have become relatively less committed to the family over the last ten years. While women have made inroads into previously male fields like the

> *Feminism has led to a mushrooming of frustrated ambition among a younger generation, particularly in single women*

professions and the police, and into sports such as mountaineering, men have become more concerned about health and appearance and have begun to organise themselves as victims of educational and jobs failure, and discrimination.

No feminism, only feminisms

Tomorrow's women will be more different from each other than women are today – in terms of life experience, opportunities and values. There will be no women's movement – only women's movements, no feminism, only feminisms. We predict the rise of business feminism, trade union feminism, new age feminism – but their adherents will not have any automatic sense of solidarity with each other. Only 15 per cent of women now define themselves primarily by gender, fewer than define themselves by their intelligence. Although women are becoming more assertive, they are unlikely to coalesce into a single movement, and politicians, advertisers and businesses will find it increasingly hard to appeal to a 'typical' woman.

Frustration explodes?

Feminism has led to a mushrooming of frustrated ambition among a younger generation, particularly in single women. Millions of women in less skilled jobs have heightened expectations which aren't being met. Fifteen per cent of all women (3.6 million) say that they are getting a raw deal out of life, and 23 per cent (5.6 million) say that they feel angry much of the time – mainly younger women in classes D and E. Overall, 60 per cent of women say that employers are still prejudiced. We predict a harder, less compromising feminism in the workplace in the future as frustrated women learn to organise. After all, for most women in part-time, insecure jobs, the glass ceiling is irrelevant; the key is to achieve time flexibility, more security, more training and higher pay.

Traditionalism returns?

The back to basics movement is likely to gain growing support, even though it is now primarily supported by over 55s. Partly because of inadequate opportunities at work, and partly because of anxieties about childcare, growing numbers of women will want to be at home. Thirteen per cent (3.2 million) of women are working but would rather be at home – most of them under 35. Thirty-six per cent of 25 to 34-year-old women believe that family life suffers if a woman works full time. We could see the evolution of a 'cult of motherhood', and a new 'mum's movement', bolstered by new agers who choose opting out to have a family over clinging to the career ladder.

Women becoming like men

We predict the flourishing of a new generation of mannish women who will ape men's traditional behaviour by hiring male escorts and male secretaries, enjoying the power they can exert over them. They will be more hedonistic, assertive and risk taking. They will spend ever less time on house cleaning, accepting male standards of cleanliness. Thirty-one per cent of women say that they would not mind being born again as a man. The proportion of women knitting or dressmaking has fallen by 10 per cent while the proportion doing DIY has risen from 24 to 30 per cent over the course of the last decade. 16-24-year-old women's smoking has gone up 5 per cent since 1994. A quarter of football fans are now women. Women are even becoming physically more like men – with an increase in heart disease, serotonin levels and drinking, as physical consequences of their changing lifestyle. Men by contrast may be set to take over from women as the main pill poppers, suffering more from depression. They may also have other reasons to be worried. As 17 per cent of women say they 'don't get mad, they get even', we are likely to see more women in the vein of Lorena Bobbit and Sharon Stone's ice-pick-wielding killer in *Basic Instinct*.

New agers on the rise

Women are becoming increasingly attached to new age values, alternative therapies, and spirituality. Twenty-six per cent of all women say that they 'feel part of a world spirit'. Thirty-six per cent say that the most important decisions in their lives are based on emotions. Balance is becoming a general concern and environmentalism is now mainstream, at the core of British values overall. The 'new age' women, who are generally more affluent, will increasingly educate their children at home, opt out of career ladders, and provide potential allies for 'back to basics' women in championing a less work-oriented culture. However, we predict that 'downshifting' will remain relevant only to a small minority – and mainly at particular lifestages.

Flexibility and time rise up the agenda

Britain has seen a revolution in women's work – but the main institutions have failed to adapt. Forty-eight per cent of working women say that flexible working hours are their highest priority, but only a small minority of employers offer such options as term-time working and four day weeks. Eighty-six per cent of working women say that they never have time to get things done. There are only 600 workplace nurseries. We predict much bigger political pressures around issues such as parental leave and childcare, which are now largely off the political agenda in the UK in stark contrast to other countries.

Stuck in the technology ghetto?

Women are in danger of being trapped in a technology ghetto. They are significantly less confident with technology than men, and see technologies like the PC and Internet as less relevant to their lives. Only 33 per cent of women use computers at work compared to 47 per cent of men. Only 20 per cent of women see the Internet as useful, and only 4 per cent of women use the Internet at work compared to 15 per cent of men.

Women and business

Twice as many new businesses are being set up by women as by men, rapidly transforming Britain's small business culture. But women are mainly going into business for freedom. Only 15 per cent say they do it for the money, compared to 34 per cent who do it for fulfilment. But all is not rosy for women in business.

Fifty-six per cent of women managers suffer from ill health because they don't have time for exercise or a good diet. Women are becoming very cynical about companies. Sixty per cent of women over 35 are angry at companies telling lies and acting unethically. Working women in particular have become significantly more sceptical about companies over the last decade.

Women doing without men

Looking further ahead, the continued fall in the sperm count and the continuing 'oestrogen storm' mean that men's fertility will continue to fall. Coupled with medical innovations to control conception, pregnancy and birth, the implication is that by early in the next century women won't need men to produce babies.

Things that matter

The three factors that women cite as having had most influence on their lives this century are the pill, the right to vote, and the washing machine, in that order. Looking ahead to 2010, we might expect a women's football league on mainstream television, a 'mothers'

movement' with millions of members, DIY pregnancy kits as well as DIY pregnancy tests, a new generation of women cyber-billionaires, an army of 'femocrats' gaining ground in government and quangos, the first major counter-demonstration by women against a men's movement march, and a new generation of smart clothes that tell washing machines how to wash them and smart food products that instruct ovens how to cook them.

More political women?

So far women have failed to mobilise their new power at work and as consumers. Part of the reason is that their interests diverge. Their energies have been directed much more to private life and work. But we predict that over the next dozen or so years they will become more assertive. Far from feminism disappearing into a depoliticised 'post-feminism' we anticipate more politicisation in the future – whether among older traditionalist women with time on their hands campaigning against abortion or pornography, or among younger women frustrated about lack of opportunities or angry about the environment.

The end of 'men-only politics'?

We also predict that women will become more prominent in mainstream politics. Women are a majority of the electorate, and they vote more than men. But they are not happy about how the parties treat them. Seventy-five per cent of 25 to 54-year-old women are dissatisfied with the parties' records on women's issues. Indeed, 1997 could be the last general election when the agenda has been almost entirely set by men. A sharp increase in the number of women MPs in 1997, combined with growing numbers of women on local councils, in the media and business will make women much more visible in British public life. By 2010 the 'men-only' agenda of contemporary British politics will be a thing of the past.

• The above is an extract from *Tomorrow's women*, ISBN 1 898309 48 5, priced at £9.95, produced by Demos, an independent think-tank committed to radical thinking on the long-term problems facing the UK. See page 41 for address details.
© Demos
January, 1998

Wanted: a tough new law to promote women

The Blair government was yesterday challenged to introduce a 'super law' aimed at giving women a fast track to equality. Barrie Clement, Labour Editor, explains that ministers and employers may want to temper justice with considerations of cost and potential conflict.

The Equal Opportunities Commission yesterday called for a tough new law which could force employers to promote women where they had been the victims of discrimination.

Under the proposals, industrial tribunals could also demand that women were taken back into jobs

where they proved they were dismissed because of gender bias.

In a report issued as part of a three-month consultation exercise, the commission argues that employers should be ordered to continue to pay compensation as long as they

---

In some cases, it took more than a decade for women to claim equal pay

---

refuse to take corrective action. At the moment, tribunals can only order a 'one-off' payment to the aggrieved party.

While employers may contend that such a law would constitute a considerable burden and lead to conflict at the workplace, the Government may prevaricate over the EOC's main proposal for legislation, which it wants to be introduced during this parliament. It is demanding a single 'equal treatment' Act which would give women a fast track to equality. Given that women's earnings are just 80 per cent of men's, such legislation could lead to claims worth billions and ministers may feel the need to phase in such a provision.

Kamlesh Bahl, chairwoman of the commission, said legislation was a 'mess and a nightmare', with more than a dozen British laws plus European directives. There was an urgent need for a review and a major overhaul, she said.

In some cases, it took more than a decade for women to claim equal pay and with pregnancy and maternity statutes were complicated and contradictory and were a disincentive to the employment of women.

The commission's chairwoman argued that equal opportunity was a fundamental right and that both the Government and employers would see the legitimacy of a review. A new law would save them millions of pounds in legal fees and address employer's demands for 'clarity', she said.

The consultation paper, which will go to all interested individuals and organisations, calls for a fundamental change from the emphasis on fighting discrimination to promoting 'the positive right to equal treatment'. Commissioners would make employers responsible for promoting equal opportunities – another possible bone of contention – and extend protection to include cases involving sexual orientation and 'gender reassignment'.

A suggestion that might concern the armed forces, however, is the contention that sexual discrimination laws concerning the military should be amended. At the moment, the forces are allowed to discriminate in cases where they believe 'combat effectiveness' could be impaired by ensuring equality. Ms Bahl believes that the only factor to be considered in recruitment or promotion is whether the candidate has the relevant experience, qualifications and abilities.

Ms Bahl acknowledged that there had been significant changes in society since the current legislation was drawn up more than 20 years ago and that men sometimes now felt they were victims. In particular the commission was investigating the academic under-achievement of boys. *© The Independent January, 1998*

Fight against injustice

Pam Enderby became aware of the injustice of her position 11 years ago. After huge legal fees expended by the Equal Opportunities Commission and her union to win her equal pay – and a similar amount expended by the National Health Service to deny her extra money – she is still waiting for compensation.

Last summer it was finally agreed that as a speech therapist in the health service her work was of equal value to that undertaken by pharmacists and psychologists.

'After more than a decade, my friends are still wanting to know when the drinks will be on me,' she said.

Ms Enderby, 47, was paid considerably less than her male colleagues. As head of her hospital department, she found she was under very similar pressures to them. In fact she had a larger staff and a wider area of research to cover than her opposite number in the psychology department.

Part of her difficulty has been that she was invoking law which means women who perform work of 'equal value' to men should be paid the same. This law is something of a minefield. It is easier – but not without difficulty – to win equal pay for the same job.

The concept of equal value is fraught with difficulty and the NHS decided to exploit the problems to the full. However, 1,200 other cases hinge on the Enderby judgment and it could cost the health service £30m in back pay and legal costs. The EOC and the MSF union have been landed with a legal bill in excess of £100,000.

Ms Enderby's case, according to the commission, is a shining example of the Byzantine nature of present legislation and the urgent need to reform it. She has since left the health service to become professor of community rehabilitation at Sheffield University. 'The problem with a lot of female professionals is that there is a "ceiling" that is not the case in male dominated professions. Men were always expected to have a career.'

Her new job uses her expertise in speech therapy: but many of her colleagues have to leave the specialism to go into hospital management. She believes there is a potential for change under the present government. 'It was obvious that under the previous administration there was an absence of political will. Every obstacle was put in one's way.'

© The Independent January, 1998

The future: focused, flexible and female

In a world of insecure jobs, young women are infinitely better prepared. While young men are still hoping to be footballers, women are busy planning their lives from school to work, acquiring that all-important work experience at every opportunity

This is the picture presented by 2020 vision, a survey by the Industrial Society of 10,000 young Britons aged between 12 and 25, the largest study of its kind. By Nicole Veash and Jack O'Sullivan

Rebecca Jones, 22, is typical of a new breed of can-do women.

'From the age of 12 I knew that I wanted to do a classics degree. I loved Latin and I enjoyed my Greek and I focused on getting the grade to go to university.

'When I left Cambridge, while I didn't know precisely what job I wanted, I knew exactly what I wanted to get out of it. I wanted something with variety, prospects for promotion, something that was exciting, dynamic and dealt with people.' Today, she works as a strategic planner in a London advertising agency.

In contrast, Paul Dunbar, a third-year economics student at Lancaster University, has not planned his life. 'I'm very worried that I've done no work experience. I've never been taught how to deal with an office for example. I never really thought about work until this term.

'Then I saw jobs being advertised and the deadlines and I thought I'd better hurry up and think of what I want to do. It is very frightening when you have 20 applications on your desk.

'A lot of guys seem to be getting a rude awakening, when they're suddenly besieged with stuff from the careers service. Women seem to focus on what they want to do for the future. Quite a few, for example, have taken a year off in industry. They certainly study harder – they're more conscientious.'

Young women, reveals the survey, are also more in tune with economic change. They are less likely than men to expect a job for life and more likely to pick themselves up after becoming unemployed and take the type of action that will secure fresh work. So whereas men tend to wait for the right job, jobless women are more willing to get fresh qualifications and take careers advice.

Women also recognise even more than their male peers that the key skills in today's age of communication are literacy and 'getting on with people.'

'The whole communication thing,' says Rebecca Jones, 'is really important, especially as this sector in the job market is expanding. Women seem to be especially good at communicating and that is why we are getting a higher profile.'

And they are learning all the time – women recognise more than men that home is a place where they can learn skills, be it for running a home, maintaining a family.

Women also have a strong agenda for ensuring their own success at work. More than a third of women, compared with a fraction of men, expect more childcare in the workplace within 10 years. And they are fierce supporters of men taking

---

Blokes are generally more competitive than women, which can be a good thing, but we get emotionally involved with what we are doing

---

up their share of childcare – 93 per cent think men and women should take equal responsibility for caring for children.

Rigid, long hours are anathema to the new female generation who see such practices as blocking their progress. A third expect more flexible hours to be available within 10 years and half think there will be more working from home.

'Women,' says Rebecca Jones, 'are driving the way we change at work. It is all about doing what we want to do on our own terms. This is a much more progressive way of thinking and it is about flexibility in the workplace.

'If, for example, I had children and I wanted time off, I would take it and have to fit that in with my work. If I wanted to leave at five and work on my laptop I would have to do that. We do the job in the end but it doesn't have to involve taking part in the faces game, just sitting at our desks and being there to be seen.'

2020 Vision is co-ordinated by the Industrial Society.

Women have better skills for the modern world

After graduating from Bradford University, Mina Dye-Sharp, 24, became a community youth volunteer.

A lot of women realise they have got to be focused. We feel we have got to do better than men and also better than the next woman. But I don't want to get on in life just because I'm a woman. I want to succeed on merit and on my abilities.

I think we have really changed the workplace. We are better listeners than men, not so aggressive and better at seeing things from a different perspective. Women are prepared to take everyone's feelings on board. They are more team-based and democratic.

Some men I work with have tunnel vision. They can only see things one way. They seem to find it hard to compromise and their communication is quite poor, which can sometimes be frustrating.

Women are more persistent. Men just seem to give up when problems arise or they just delegate downwards. Negotiation is really important at work.

Compromising is not about giving up. You can still stand by what you believe in. Work is all about give and take.

Blokes are generally more competitive than women, which can be a good thing, but we get emotionally involved with what we are doing.

Women are more persistent. Men just seem to give up when problems arise or they just delegate downwards

---

Women are more realistic about the job market in the future. We know that we are the only ones who can make things happen.

Men just say the opportunities are not out there. I think the problem is that young men don't have a traditional role and that is why women appear to be so much more focused. Men need to realise they have an important part to play in society. I've got a lot of single mothers as friends who are all going back to higher education. They feel they have missed out and that is the only way for them to get off income support. They need to help themselves and they are very focused on that.

It's no longer important to marry or settle down and have a child. If a man doesn't stick around after a baby is born, women aren't that bothered any more. We can cope without a man around and it's less hassle.

There is onus on young women to succeed and do more. Even that girl-power thing is like peer pressure. The media is telling women that they have got to go further and do better, so in the end being a career-oriented woman could be like conforming to a modern stereotype.

© The Independent
November, 1997

Women and employment

Information from the Fawcett Society

Women at work in the 1990s

'I want a career that is stimulating and satisfying and paid at the same rates as men'

In the 1990s the vast majority of women of working age without children are in paid employment and an increasing number of mothers remain in the workplace when they have children. However this does not mean that women are 'taking over' from men at work.

In early 1996 there were 12.3 million men working full-time compared with only 6.1 million women, with male employment rising faster than female employment. A further 4.8 million women are working part-time and of these 1.8 million work less than 16 hours a week.

Children have the biggest impact on women's working lives. Most women have a period of full-time work followed by part-time work and many have a period out of the workforce returning to work longer hours or full-time when their children are grown up.

What kind of work do women do?

'I want an end to the job stereotyping and second class status of work done by women'

Three-quarters of people working in clerical, secretarial and health occupations are women.

The present workforce is still divided on gender lines. Women mainly work in a few sectors, clerical and secretarial, personal service occupations, sales, health and education and tend to be found in the less senior posts. The small number of men in these sectors tend to be found in more senior positions.

Men still predominate in industry and craft occupations, the police, engineering and construction and in senior posts in all sectors.

Change is happening, for example, women are now entering the 'traditional' professions in increasing numbers and make up around one-third of solicitors. However women and men are often still encouraged into traditional job choices by schools and career services.

Policy change – to promote positive strategies in career services and schools to overcome gender stereotyping.

What do women earn?

'I am tired of earning less than many men who aren't so skilled as I am'

In all sectors and at all levels the average man earns more per hour than the average woman.

Twenty years after the introduction of the Equal Pay Act there is still an estimated £20 billion pay gap between women and men. The equal pay law is complex. If women win cases, this benefits them as individuals and does not extend to other women in similar situations. The procedures are very expensive and often take years to complete.

Policy change – to strengthen the legislation on equal pay for work of equal value so that it works quickly and effectively.

During the past 20 years a wide range of equal pay cases have been won:

- administrators have won equal pay with car cleaners,
- checkout operators with warehousemen,
- dinner ladies with road sweepers.

Equal pay cases have shown that work traditionally done by women is under-valued and as a result underpaid.

Policy change – to implement the EOC Code of Practice on Equal Pay to remove bias against women's jobs in all government and state-funded employment. Necessary pay changes should be implemented by the year 2000.

What hours do women work?

'I am exhausted at the end of the day. I want time for family, friends and life!'

Professional women under 24 work the longest hours of any occupation and any age group, seven hours more each week than young male professionals (Demos).

A culture of 'presenteism', where people have to be seen to be in their workplaces for long hours, prevents both women and men from leading balanced lives. This creates barriers for women who still have the main responsibility for childcare and prevents men from enjoying their share of family and domestic responsibilities.

Policy change – to implement the European Commission Directives on working time to eliminate the long hours culture and set an example of good practice in government and state-funded jobs.

'I want recognition that I work as hard as a full-time worker, if not harder'

Over 6 million women work part-time and over half give domestic and family commitments as the reason for their choice.

The availability of part-time work is important to many women but this does not mean that such work is unimportant to them. Women do not want their part-time work to be low status, low paid and with no possibility of promotion. It is unjust that women's commitment to their families should be used to undermine their value in the workplace.

Policy change – to ensure equal terms and conditions, including promotion and access to training for part-time workers.

Is flexible work woman friendly?

'I want flexible hours and career breaks without being regarded as uncommitted'

One in three women under 34 would like a job that allowed them to only work during term time (Demos).

Women often benefit from flexible working. Job-sharing can open up jobs which have traditionally only been available full-time to those that wish to work part-time. Term-time working allows parents to work when children are at school but not during school holidays. However employers are often unwilling to allow employees to change to more flexible working patterns. Only 3% of women employees are job-sharing. 10% of part-time workers work term-times only.

Policy change – to encourage job-sharing, annual hours and term-time working at all levels in local and national government and promote information about the value of family-friendly employment.

A typical employee on a 'flexible' zero hours contract does not know from one week to the next how many hours or on what days they will be working and therefore how much they will earn or when they will need childcare.

Not all 'flexible' work contracts benefit women. There is a growing trend towards zero hours contracts where employees have to be available for work at any time but are not given any guarantee of work. Under such conditions it is impossible for working mothers to plan their childcare. Family life is disrupted and there is insecurity of income. It is hard to see any benefits to the worker from zero hours contracts.

Policy change – to ban zero hours contracts and to lower the qualifying period for employment rights from two years to six months.

Childcare is a key issue for most working parents. Fawcett supports the development of a strategy to provide affordable quality childcare for all who need it as outlined in the Manifesto of the Childcare Alliance.

Action for a better deal for women at work

We want the Government to:

- Promote the strategies in career services and schools to overcome gender stereotyping
- Improve the equal pay laws
- Re-evaluate the pay and status of traditional 'women's' jobs
- Implement the European Commission Directive to limit working hours
- Ensure equal terms and conditions for part-time workers
- Encourage positive flexible working
- Ban zero hours contracts

• The above is information from the Fawcett Society. See page 41 for address details. © *Fawcett Society*

Key facts and guidance for managers

Information on equal opportunities from the Industrial Society

Definition

Equal opportunities is removing barriers to access and opportunity, and managing diversity with positive results for individuals and organisations.

- It refers to equality in recruitment, promotion, training or transfer, terms and conditions of employment, and dismissal – not discriminating on grounds of race, ethnic origin, sex, marital status, sexual orientation, religion, culture, class, age, disability, medical record, or any other factor irrelevant to ability to do the job.

Background

- Until the 1970s there was no law in the UK on equality of opportunity other than the Disabled Persons (Employment) Acts of 1944 and 1958 which established a three per cent 'quota' system, and some designated 'employments' for disabled people.
- the first [equal pay] legislation was driven by the UK's obligation under Article 119 of the Treaty of Rome to 'ensure and subsequently maintain the application of the principle that men and women should receive equal pay for equal work', which now also includes work of equal value.
- Subsequently, the EEC's 'Equal Treatment' Directive of 1975 expanded the principle of equality to outlaw discrimination on grounds of sex in working conditions, selection criteria, access to jobs, and all levels of the occupational hierarchy.
- The Race Relations Act of 1976 extended anti-discrimination law by providing similar protection to people discriminated against on grounds of race.

Key facts

The CRE survey *Large companies and racial equality* reveals that while 88 per cent of large companies have a policy on race discrimination, only 45 per cent have an action plan in place.

- Department for Education and Employment figures suggest that 40 per cent of employers practise age discrimination in recruitment, training and promotion.
- Observation [backed by government statistics] shows that in many organisations, female employees are still concentrated in the lowest-paid jobs, and the proportion of women in senior management posts is still disproportionately low.
- DFEE figures [1994] indicate that full-time women earn 78.8 per cent of the hourly rate paid to full-time men. Many women are concentrated in part-time low-paid jobs.

Key legislation in the UK is:

- The Equal Pay Act 1970
- The Sex Discrimination Act 1975
- The Race Relations Act 1976
- The Disability Discrimination Act 1995
- The Rehabilitation of Offenders Act 1974
- The Fair Employment Acts [Northern Ireland]

State of play

There is no legislation forbidding discrimination on sexual orientation or age [though occasionally such discrimination may fall under one of the anti-discrimination Acts]; nor, outside Northern Ireland, against religion or political affiliation.

- Discrimination may be direct or indirect. Indirect discrimination occurs when a requirement or condition applied has a disproportionately adverse effect on one sex or group. Discrimination is unlawful even where there is no intention to discriminate.
- Organisations are, however, allowed to undertake positive action programmes to overcome under-representation of a particular sex or race.
- There are three statutory bodies dealing with sex, race and disability discrimination respectively – the Equal Oppor-

tunities Commission [EOC], the Commission for Racial Equality [CRE], and the National Disability Council. Unlike the others, the NDC will not have powers of enforcement.

- The Disability Discrimination Act 1995 [due to come into effect in 1996] provides protection against discrimination on grounds of disability and the Rehabilitation of Offenders Act 1974 on grounds of spent offences. In Northern Ireland, the Fair Employment Acts prevent discrimination on grounds of religion and political affiliation, though some religious discrimination may fall within the ambit of the Race Relations Act [such as discrimination against Jews and Sikhs].

- The European Union has produced a Code on the Dignity of Men and Women at Work, with the aim of preventing sexual harassment. This is taken into account in harassment claims, even though it is not a statutory code.

Best practice guidelines

Equality is about good management practice, helping businesses to deliver a more efficient and cost-effective service.

- By removing barriers to access and opportunity employers can tap into a broader pool of valuable skills and potential.
- Failure to manage diversity

effectively can be costed – in terms of employee turnover and absence, lost business, lack of competitiveness, and even compensation awards in industrial tribunals.

- Equal opportunities is not a 'bolt-on' luxury. It should be embodied in the organisation's mission statement and in its strategy – it needs to be incorporated within the policies and rolling business plan of the organisation.

- Draw up an equal opportunities statement incorporating all the factors on which discrimination might be based. Set out good practice standards in recruitment, promotion, training, transfer, pay and conditions of work. Integrate these principles into all your policies and communicate your approach to all employees.

- Provide training on the organisation's philosophy and practice in the provision of equal opportunity.

- Offer pre-employment training where appropriate, and take other positive action issues faced by under-represented groups.

- Monitor progress in achieving the objectives of the policy. Review recruitment, selection, promotion and training procedures regularly.

- Draw up clear, accurate job descriptions and person specifications.

- Consider flexible working, career breaks, childcare facilities, etc.

- Develop links with local community groups, other employers' organisations and schools.

- Be aware of your organisation's image amongst its shareholders, customers, suppliers, staff and within the community.

Industrial society help

A wide range of public and in-house training courses in managing diversity and women's development is available.

Relevant publications include:
- *Managing Best Practice* No 14, Managing Diversity;
- *Equal Opportunities* training pack/video covering sex and race discrimination, disabilities and sexual harassment;
- *Equal opportunities, a practical handbook* by Gill Taylor;
- *A Guide to the Employment Acts* by Joan Henderson.

- The above is an extract from *Equal Opportunities*, a factsheet produced by the Industrial Society. See page 41 for address details.

© The Industrial Society
June, 1998

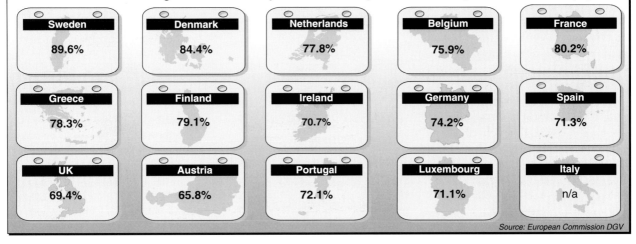

The earnings gap

**Average hourly earnings of female manual workers as a percentage of male manual workers, 1994.
In no country of the EU are earnings for manual workers equal between men and women; in most countries women doing manual work are paid about three quarters the average amount of men's pay.**

Sweden	Denmark	Netherlands	Belgium	France
89.6%	84.4%	77.8%	75.9%	80.2%

Greece	Finland	Ireland	Germany	Spain
78.3%	79.1%	70.7%	74.2%	71.3%

UK	Austria	Portugal	Luxembourg	Italy
69.4%	65.8%	72.1%	71.1%	n/a

Source: European Commission DGV

Sex and shopping

Why women still get a raw deal when it comes to paying

Women can no longer be charged more than men in New York for items such as haircuts and dry cleaning, after the city authority outlawed 'gender pricing'. But here in Britain, women still pay more than men for many everyday services. Glenda Cooper, Social Affairs Correspondent, and Rosa Prince investigate why there's no such thing as a cheap woman.

Sex and shopping have long been linked in most women's minds, but never quite so literally. New York City has followed California in outlawing gender discrimination in pricing.

Put simply this means hairdressing salons will be unable to have prices which distinguish between men and women or face a $500 (£300) fine. The same goes for dry cleaners who can no longer charge more for a blouse than a shirt.

However, here in Britain, it's still hard to be a woman. Technically section 29 of the Sex Discrimination Act outlaws gender discrimination on goods and services. In practice, a spokeswoman explains it can be difficult to prove. 'Many shops charge women higher prices because they say it costs more in labour and overheads. It's very difficult to prove. Manufacturers and retailers say different prices for men and women are due to different costs in manufacturing or provision of services and so the Sex Discrimination Act is unlikely to apply.'

A spokeswoman from the Consumers' Association said that they had done no research into the area of gender pricing but added that she felt 'it should be part of our agenda'.

Ray Seymour, general secretary of the National Hairdressers' Federation, countered yesterday that higher prices in the salon were

justified. 'The basic situation is that it does cost more to cut ladies' hair than men's,' he said.

'Most ladies' hair is below the ears, is longer than men's and needs more styling. In the same way, the cost of cutting a bald man's hair is the same as anyone else even though he has less hair.'

Introducing similar measures in Britain he feels would be disastrous: 'You can get more men passing over a seat than women in an hour. So if you're only cutting women's hair you have fewer customers. It would hit the salons hard. They couldn't afford to bring the prices down so they would charge men as much as women and end up penalising men. Why does everything have to be PC these days?'

Still there is evidence that in some areas prices are evening out – for example in dry cleaning. Alan Maycock, of Jeeves of Belgravia, said yesterday: 'Years ago there were

---

Where women tend to get their own back is car insurance, with young women sometimes getting quotes which are £100 less than young men

---

circumstances when the cost of cleaning a lady's shirt was greater than a man's. But the ladies complained and most dry cleaners now charge the same.'

Where women tend to get their own back is car insurance, with young women sometimes getting quotes which are £100 less than young men. The reasons women are considered a safer bet is because men under 40 are twice as likely as women to drive without due or reasonable care and attention and twice as likely to break the speed limit.

'Young women behave rather differently than young men when they get behind a steering wheel,' said David Steven of Admiral Insurance.

'Young men have much higher numbers of driving convictions and more claims per person. And when they do crash it tends to be much harder than when young women do, so the claim is more.'

Miranda Seymour of Direct Line added: 'The difference in the rate we charge for men and women is all based on experience. Our experience is that females in the younger age groups make fewer claims. By about the age of 40, the difference between the two has evened out.'

There are some areas where women may still win out, like 'ladies' nights' in pubs and clubs where women get subsidised drinks to attract their (civilising) custom, but even this is dying out. A spokesman for the Brewers' and Licensed Retailers' Association said: 'That sort of thing has gone out like the old rules that a woman had to be seated or that they wouldn't serve a woman wearing trousers. Certainly I'm not aware that it ever happens in pubs now.'

© The Independent
January, 1998

Militant men declare war on 'social evil of feminism'

By Barrie Clement,
Labour Editor

An organisation for militant males – denounced as a group of 'sad misogynists' by its critics – is bombarding the Equal Opportunities Commission with complaints about the treatment of men.

A group of activists belonging to the United Kingdom Men's Movement is intent on 'gumming up the works', according to commission officials.

The movement is fighting feminism which it regards as 'the greatest social evil of our time' and calling for the abolition of the commission and the repeal of equal rights legislation.

Members of the Men's Movement have embarked on a campaign to inundate the commission with calls urging action over a series of alleged iniquities which serve to undermine the role of men.

Officials at the commission are frustrated by the onslaught because some of the complaints have substance. However, officials are also aware of the organisation's aim to destroy the commission.

'There might come a stage when the public service requirement – whereby the commission is duty-bound to respond in detail to inquiries – becomes ridiculous,' said one source close to the commission.

> ## The movement is fighting feminism which it regards as 'the greatest social evil of our time'

The Men's Movement's latest broadside against 'political correctness' came yesterday when it attacked a decision to abolish the lower height limit for firefighters in Northern Ireland because it amounted to indirect discrimination against women.

The commission had pointed out that more women were below the height of 5ft 6in than men.

The men's group yesterday issued a statement pointing out that the maximum height requirement of 6ft 4in discriminated against men because there were more of them above that height.

George McAulay, of the Men's Movement, yesterday argued that height was an important ingredient in assessing whether someone was capable of doing the job.

He said his organisation, of which he is Scottish chairman, formed the 'shock troops in the campaign for men's equality'. He contended that men suffered discrimination over employment, pensions and divorce. Unmarried fathers had few rights as far as their children were concerned, he said.

Critics of the Men's Movement, which is funded by a claimed membership of 'a couple of thousand', argue that its membership varies from intelligent, rational individuals to 'nasty people with chips on their shoulders'.

Some members have allegedly been abusive on the telephone to officials at the commission and have been told that their inquiries and communications will only be dealt with by letter.

© *The Independent*
February, 1997

REFUSE TO MAKE THE TEA? – YOU'RE NOT ONE OF THESE DAMNED FEMINISTS ARE YOU, MISS TIMPSON?

KenPyne

Discrimination against men

Information from the Cambridge Men's Action Group

Health

Men die on average 7 years earlier than women. Before the age of 65 men are three times as likely to suffer heart disease and twice as likely to die from lung cancer than women. Women visit their doctors around twice as often as men, and women form the majority of patients treated in hospital. It seems men can do more to help themselves as they leave serious medical conditions too late by not visiting the doctor. Men make-up the majority of accident and emergency cases. More men drive and for longer distances so they are involved in the majority of road traffic accidents. Since men work in dangerous occupations they suffer the majority of industrial accidents. Men drink three times more and smoke at a slightly greater rate than women. Men do seem to have a built-in self-destruct mechanism, and although nearly all medical advances have been made by men, it seems the last person that men will help is themselves.

Screening programmes are provided for women-related cancers such as breast and cervical cancer. However there is no screening of equivalent cancers affecting men such as prostate and testicular cancer. This is very unfair because deaths from prostate cancer are almost as high as deaths from breast cancer and 6.7 times higher than deaths from cervical cancer. The bias is further tilted because research spending overwhelmingly is in favour of women cancers. The most up-to-date health targets for the UK include: B1 – reduction of breast cancer by 25%, and B2 – reduction of cervical cancer by 20%. There is not even a mention of prostate, or testicular cancer targets. Men need to demand that more is spent on male health and prevention programmes.

Health leaflets published by the NHS and other groups are available in doctors' surgeries. Many of these

leaflets target women only issues such as breast and cervical cancer. Visitors to doctors' surgeries in the UK will be hard pressed to find even a single leaflet targeting men-only conditions. Some of the leaflets are obviously pursuing an 'agenda'. The leaflet *Your Health: A guide to services for women* published by the Department of Health has a whole page on domestic violence: 'Domestic violence includes emotional, as well as sexual or physical abuse of women in their homes by partners.' It then goes on to give the phone number of women's aid and rape crisis lines. This is classic 'male-bashing' in its purest form. The leaflet makes no mention that serious studies into this area have shown that women are more likely to commit domestic violence against their partners or children. The leaflet contains no phone numbers to help men who experience domestic violence, or to help women who are abusive or violent to their male partners.

Public libraries

Libraries are beginning the apartheid practices of excluding men. Libraries do this by having women-only library tables, or women-only library days. However these services are paid for by revenues that we all pay for. In Leicester, the County Council is being legally challenged over this issue, and taken to court. The council will be contesting this issue in court so demonstrating a deliberate will to impose this discrimination.

Libraries are staffed mainly by women and therefore there is an automatic tendency to stock information that favours women. As an example the Cambridge main library information service has computer searches giving details of local groups. Entering the key word 'women' gave about 50 references, typing in 'men' gave 0 references. The library acted swiftly to correct this obvious gender imbalance. A second example was that the library had a 'women's issues' shelf but no 'men's issues' shelf. Again the library acted swiftly to correct this imbalance and with the help of donated books a men's shelf was soon available. This suggests that there was no real intentional bias and that maybe libraries are 'demand-led'.

Radio

Radio 4, the main national serious radio station has a women's hour, but does not have a men's hour. Although the women's hour programme has moved beyond the mantra of 'all men are rapists and abusers' the program regularly features guests who are of this ilk. Equality must cut both ways. Controversial feminist views and skewed statistics are allowed onto the airwaves unopposed. Radio 4 therefore needs to also have a programme where men are equally able to complain about women. Here is an example of how men's issues are mistreated by Radio 4 on the *Today* programme.

'... *During yesterday's broadcast she (Anna Ford) introduced an item on the treatment of men during divorce cases. There were two participants: Elizabeth Woodcraft a feminist barrister, and Neil Lyndon, author of the uncompromisingly anti-feminist No More Sex War. Lyndon felt that the interview was rather skewed in favour of his opponent, who was allowed to talk for more than two of the piece's three minutes. After the broadcast he received a call from Today's deputy editor, Rod Little, agreeing, apologising and saying Miss Ford had been reprimanded ...*'

Sunday Telegraph 31 Sep 97

The BBC World Service has traditionally had a reputation for excellence. The station features news and documentaries with reporters of world standing such as Mark Tully and Misha Glenny. A recent drive is under way to feminise the World Service (announcement: 'calling all our women listeners' BBC 13 Aug 96): a new programme called *Everywoman* targets women listeners and copies the Radio 4 *Woman's Hour* practice of including a liberal sprinkling of male-bashing. New World Service reporters such as Julliet Tindell now send back reports from Tokyo (BBC 26 Aug 96) where for example women are illegally imported into Japan to work in the 'entertainment' industry as prostitutes. According to the Japanese newspaper *The Yomiuri Shimbun* Mon 12 Aug 1996 there are 160,836 male and 123,664 female immigrants staying illegally in Japan as estimated by the Ministry of Law (1 May 96).

The men work in the so-called KKK jobs. In Japanese KKK stands for dangerous, hard, and dirty, i.e. the jobs that no Japanese would want to do. The BBC programme failed to mention anything about the fate of these illegal male immigrants. The programme also failed to mention anything about men imported to work as male prostitutes. It is tempting to suggest that if immigrant women to Japan were being burnt to death in blast furnaces, or being trapped under agricultural machinery then we would soon hear about it from Tindell. This pattern of 'women-as-victim' reporting is increasingly repeated in many other countries by the BBC World Service. The new correspondents have an obvious 'male-bashing' agenda and this is excluding the highly respected and experienced correspondents such as Tully and Glenny.

Marriage

At present 75% of all divorces are called for by wives. *The Emperor's New Clothes* survey of divorced men found that a man pays £29,306 to his lawyers and transfers £57,966 to his wife of which she then pays £20,000 to her lawyers. Thus lawyers benefit by £49,306 on average per divorce. If a man takes the step of marrying and has children:

- He has a 50/50 chance of: divorcing, losing custody of his children and paying £87,272 (avg)
- He will have a 1 in 3 chance of losing his home

- He will have a 1 in 10 chance of losing contact with his children for ever

If a women takes the step of marrying and has children:

- It is almost certain she will keep her children
- She will also have a 1 in 3 chance of losing her home
- Have a 50/50 chance she will benefit by £37,966 (average)

Lifestyle opportunities

Women have multiple lifestyle opportunities versus men's single opportunity i.e. work. At present women have the option to:

- Work
- Stay at home as a housewife
- Stay home with children
- Work part time and care for children part time

Education

Our education system and especially our primary education system is betraying a whole generation of boy pupils [*Mail* 13 Sep 95]. A leading American educationalist, Spencer Holland, blamed in particular a lack of male teachers in primary schools. His quick-fix solution was to send men into the schools to act as mentors and role models to male pupils. A recent international literacy survey found that more than a fifth of adults in the UK, i.e. some 8 million people, could not perform simple comprehension tests. This places the UK second to last, i.e. above Poland but below Germany, Holland, Sweden, Switzerland, US, and Canada (*Mail* 12 Sep 97).

There are 4.7 times as many female teachers in primary (aged 5-13 years) schools compared to male teachers. In secondary schools (aged 13-18 years) the teacher ratio is about even. It is often stated that there are no male teachers at the primary level because the pay is so bad. This is only half the story, there are now many unemployed male teachers. It is still an accepted prejudice by men and women that the raising of young children is 'women's work'.

UK schools have many barriers to involvement by fathers. Some fathers report that they are excluded by other mothers when they collect their children. The school timetable is not helpful to fathers who work, there are frequent holidays that may not coincide with the father's own holidays. The school may often be sited an inconvenient distance away from where men traditionally work.

Access courses are 'back to work' initiatives for mainly mothers paid for by government. So while funding is being withdrawn from our brightest university students who now have to 'pay as they go', mothers receive free entitlement to be educated not once but twice.

Women's 'resource centres' receive generous local and EEC funding. For example the Cambridge Women's Resource Centre currently receives £250,000 a year grant to offer training courses to women that exclude men. Many of these women-only courses are provided in areas of record male unemployment which is often three times the unemployment rate of women. Such apartheid practices in South Africa provoked an international boycott.

Employment

Men in full-time employment work an average of 41.9 hours per week compared to women's 37.6 hours per week. More men than women work. However the unemployment rate for men at 14% is currently about three times the female rate. Traditional industries that have employed men are being closed such as mining and ship-building. Nothing is being done to restore the wealth-creating manufacturing industry, which would employ men.

Men also take on jobs that are hard, dangerous, and dirty. Industrial injuries at work are overwhelmingly of men. It is very rare to see women working as street cleaners or refuse collectors. These are the so-called glass cellar jobs, i.e. jobs that women seem not to want.

Passports

An unmarried man cannot apply for a passport for a child unless he has the permission of the mother. This means that an unmarried father is unable to take his own children on any foreign holidays. A mother does not need the father's permission to apply for a passport since nationality

The school timetable is not helpful to fathers who work, there are frequent holidays that may not coincide with the father's own holidays

for children of unmarried parents is via the mother.

Despite repeated applications to the Equal Opportunities Commission, a body that has been specifically set up to redress discrimination, they have refused to assist in this matter.

Newspapers

Newspapers regularly feature articles by such journalists as Polly Toynbee (*Independent*) that whine about men. The newspapers do have a press complaints body but these complaints will only be accepted if you are personally mentioned in the article or the complaint is perceived to be in the public interest. For example, one recent complaint the Press Complaints Commission received was about two articles in the *Yorkshire Evening Post*: 'Battle to free child snatcher – sentence on dad too harsh, says campaign' (8 Mar 96) and 'Court ruling looms – Mum in fight for children' (4 Jan 96). The father and the mother both committed the same offence. They travelled with their children to another country against a court order. Same offence, different headline in the newspaper, and completely different tone in the body of the text. The reply stated:

' . . . Only in exceptional circumstances a complaint from a third party may be investigated should the Commission consider that a significant issue involving the public interest is raised . . . the Commissioners do not find your complaint raises such an issues under the Code.'

Obviously the fate of 45,000 fathers who lose all contact with their children every year is not considered a significant issue. It is according to the press acceptable to present a mother as a heroine and a father as a child snatcher.

Advertising

Advertisements regularly feature men as foolish. The main aim of the advertisers is to appeal to women who control and make the majority of purchases. There has been a recent disturbing trend of using images of violence against men to sell products to young women (*Sunday Telegraph* 14 Sep 97).

The car company Nissan recently placed advertisements in women's magazines for a car called the Micra targeting younger women who make up 70 per cent of the car's buyers. The heading was 'Hate Male'. The advertisement encourages women readers to write in and get sent postcard pictures of a man who had been compromised by a woman after he had borrowed her car without asking. The pictures are: A man bent in agony holding his crutch, a man's jacket in tatters with both arms cut off, a male watch being fried in a pan, a man sleeping with half his hair and beard cut off, a woman holding a can of opened dog food behind her back and in the background a man is sitting eating, a paper clipping lying on a table of the Bobbit case entitled: A night to dismember, and a book with the last few pages cut out.

In an advertisement on television by Volkswagen a divorcing husband tries to claim that his VW car is worth a great deal more money than it really is. The wife discovers this overvaluation and gets her own back on the husband by 'taking him to the cleaners'. The wife is seen crowing over her victory and thanking VW for their cheapness. The husband is left standing at the kerb and gets his clothes back from the cleaners torn to shreds (presumably by his wife).

A billboard advertisement for Lee jeans features a naked man lying on the floor. A women wearing Lee jeans is shown with her stiletto above the man's buttocks. The caption reads 'Put the boot it'.

An advertisement for Wallis clothes, featuring in women's magazines, shows men about to be killed because they are staring at women. In one, a man is about to have his throat cut because his barber is staring at a pretty girl.   ©*B. Robertson, Cambridge Men's Action Group*

Gene wars

Meet man's new boss. She's psychologically and physically stronger, has massive genetic advantages and is poised to take over the world. *Focus* takes you face to face with your Amazonian future. By Jo Carlowe

This is the mid 21st century. The great head-to-head confrontation between the sexes has been won by women. Your boss, a graduate of a women-only college – the most prestigious academic institution in the country – calls you into her office. She's not happy with your typing speed, the coffee's cold . . . and if you do it again she'll rip you to shreds in front of your colleagues in the male typing pool.

An unlikely scenario? Well perhaps not. Right now women are out-performing men on every front: in education, at home, at work, in the mating game and even in what were once the most sacred, male-dominated territories of business, the Armed Forces and sport.

Men simply underestimated the competition. It's no longer a Man's World and anyone who still thinks it is (including James Brown) is wrong. If the world naturally belongs to anyone it's to women. Scientific evidence shows they are both psychologically and physically stronger than men. At school, girls are hammering the boys in exams. Test and exam results last year showed girls were way ahead of boys right through school, from the age of seven up to 16. Studies show that boys also fall behind girls in their ability to read, to concentrate and to cope with tricky situations, as well as in productivity, self-esteem and social skills. Girls are much better at persevering than boys.

In the workplace women have adapted well to the changing job market, whereas men have singly failed to face up to reality. And if you thought, charitably, women might merely be as good as men in business, think again. They are on top and they deserve to be there. Tests carried out by Lawrence A Praff and Associates in December 1996 discovered that women had outscored their male colleagues in 15 out of 20 categories including major areas such as goal setting, planning and decisiveness.

Not giving us a sporting chance

Even in the traditionally male-dominated arena of sporting achievement women are showing their mettle. Recently, all-women teams have sailed right around the world, trekked to the South Pole and climbed Mount Everest.

If women wanted to it would seem that they could outdo men in just about any sphere they chose. Earlier this year the Royal Navy appointed two women to command warships. Even in gambling, that most hotly contested male proving ground, it is women who are the most astute punters – as revealed by a recent study on horse race betting that formed part of a broader study of gender differences in leisure activity by Alistair Bruce and Johnnie Johnson at the University of Nottingham.

At least men can be smug in the knowledge they are fitter and healthier than women – can't they? Actually, it seems not. Women body-builders have shown that they can attain muscles which ripple every bit as impressively as men's. And they benefit just as much from physical training as men.

In fact a sports science study conducted in Sweden has shown that women's bodies are better at using fat, which enables them to outstrip men in endurance exercises. Chuck a man and a woman into the Atlantic Ocean on a cold day and the woman's distribution of fat will help her to survive for longer than the man.

Men tend to put on fat around their waists due to the male androgen hormones. This makes them apple shaped. Women are more pear shaped due to an oestrogen dominance. Apple-shaped people have a higher risk of heart disease and blood sugar problems such as diabetes. This goes some way to explaining why women live for an average of five years longer than men. The life expectancy for men is just 73.9 years. For women it is 79.2 years.

Men have more accidents than women (the second highest cause of death in 18 to 25-year-old men). They take more drugs and are four times as likely to commit suicide than women (the main cause of death in young men).

This is due in part to the male hormone, testosterone, which is the physiological basis of violent and impulsive behaviour. Testosterone helps develop sexual differentiation between a male and female foetus in the womb. A biological feedback system increases its levels in males, triggering development of male sexual characteristics that include differences in the development of the brain, specifically the hypo-thalamus. Absence of testosterone at this stage of prenatal development, in the third and fourth months of pregnancy, ensures the foetus is female.

In the singles stakes men don't appear to be surviving so well either, whereas women are fine. Fewer are getting married – and with good reason. The US Census Bureau counted three million unmarried over 35-year-olds in 1984 and 4.5 million by 1994.

They want to be alone . . .

In *Flying Solo: Single Women in Midlife* by family therapists Carol Anderson, Susan Stewart and Sona Dimidjian, it was found that many of these women were happy with their lot. And with some justification. 'Men generally do better physically, mentally, and career-wise when married and the reverse for women. Surveys suggest women live longer, are happier and accomplish more professionally when single.'

Women have less use for men, but men need women more than ever. Single men are three times more likely to suffer a mental disorder than their married counterparts, according to a study that was published in the *American Journal of Sociology and Health*. And those who are married need pampering.

An American insurance company found that men whose wives had kissed them before they drove off to work were half as likely to be in a crash than their unpecked counterparts.

And as if to really rub it in, advertising companies have started to capitalise on woman power with advertisements showing down-trodden men in such a degrading light that a significant number went crying to the Advertising Standards Authority.

The Lee jeans advert showed a man stamped into the ground by a woman, with the caption 'Put the boot in'. Seventy-seven people complained to the ASA about sexism and violence against men. The Nissan Micra advertisement, 'Ask before you borrow', which featured a man clutching his groin in agony, also caused a stir. Neither complaint was upheld, which inevitably led to accusations of double standards. 'It is not the ASA that is creating double standards, it is society at large,' explained an ASA spokesman.

But, hey. Don't get mad – get

An Australian study revealed that the part of the brain used for speech and language was 20-30 per cent larger in women than in men

---

even. You can't do everything about losing the sex wars, but you don't have to just sit there and take it. It all comes down to how many gender differences are innate and how many are learnt – the old nature versus nurture conundrum.

The reason for this male-female reversal of fortune is a combination of social, environmental and genetically predetermined factors, leaving men with the ability to change some things but not others. The bad news for men is that the latest research has come to the conclusion that the differences in social skills and behaviour have more to do with genetics than scientists previously believed.

What differentiates a man's genetic material from a woman's is the presence of a Y sex chromosome coupled with an X sex chromosome – in women both sex chromosomes are X. This Y chromosome has been passed from the man's father, as it is the sperm which determines the sex of a fertilised egg (if it's carrying an X, it's a girl; and if it's a Y, it's a boy). So the X chromosome of a boy is always received from his mother; on the other hand a girl has an X chromosome from both her father and mother.

Genetic headstart over the boys

Research into a genetic disorder called Turner's Syndrome, which can affect sexual development and growth and can cause problems with social adjustment, has shown that boys actually get a raw deal with their XY genetic set-up. Girls with Turner's Syndrome only have one sex chromosome, an X either from their father or mother, making it possible to study the difference between the two.

It was through pursuing such a

---

study that David Skuse, professor of behavioural science at the Institute of Child Health in London, came across evidence that girls have a genetic headstart on boys. He found that Turner Syndrome girls who had inherited their X chromosome from their mother showed worse symptoms of the disorder than those who had inherited it from their father.

It is the father's X chromosome which switches on feminine intuition in a girl before she is born, thereby equipping her with better social skills. 'This means that men have to learn social skills while women simply pick them up intuitively,' Professor Skuse says.

Boys are deprived of this intuition and have to make do with their mother's X chromosome which, as with Turner Syndrome girls, could explain why they are more likely to develop speech disorders, language impairment, reading disabilities as well as the more severe social disorders such as autism.

Skuse suggests that the evolutionary advantage to men of being socially insensitive was once to enable them to hunt and fight. In prehistoric times men had to draw away from the cave community to brave the far reaches of the wild where natural selection favoured hardened senses and superhuman strength.

These finely evolved traits served men perfectly well around 40,000 years ago. But their residue in the caring, hugging Nineties, where emotional sensitivity is rewarded and macho behaviour slapped down, can leave men feeling wrongly equipped for the modern world around them. Social skills and communication are now the order of the day, not brute force.

Women have a further advantage in communicating through the way they use their brains. An Australian study revealed that the part of the brain used for speech and language was 20-30 per cent larger in women than in men, taking into account the overall difference in size. It is an anatomical explanation of why women do better in tests on verbal fluency, verbal memory and some fine motor skills.

A second study carried out at

Yale University School of Medicine used a magnetic resonance MRI scanner to show that men only use the left side of the brain to deal with difficult linguistic problems while women use both sides. This goes some way to explaining why women are better than men on tests of linguistic ability.

It may also explain why women are better at emotional communication. Although the left hemisphere of the brain controls speech, the right hemisphere contributes to its emotional content – tests carried out on people who have suffered damage to the right side have shown that they speak without emotion.

The ability of women to use both sides of their brain at once when communicating enables them to access emotional centres at the same time as speaking. Men, on the other hand, do not have this ability to express their feelings with ease. A whole spate of psychological studies back this up, showing that women express feelings, including love and sadness, more often and more clearly than men.

We're not on speaking terms

This difference in the way men and women use their brains creates misunderstandings within relationships. Not only is there an obvious imbalance in the way each expresses the way they feel about the other. But conversations are also conducted in a very different way by men and women. Women like to explore every aspect of an issue, not necessarily needing to make a specific point, whereas men like to get straight to the point and will often become impatient with endless women's chat.

Kostas Kafetsios, a psychologist with an interest in emotional communication, believes it is a man's inability to express what he feels that causes many relationship problems.

'It suggests men's emotions are hard to decipher, presenting extra problems in relationships. Especially with typical relationship patterns where you have an avoidant (non-expressive) male with an over-expressive and sometimes anxious female,' he said. He puts this phenomenon down to socialisation

with boys learning to inhibit their emotions more than girls.

Ian Banks, a GP specialising in men's health, also believes the answer to men's problems comes down to social expectations rather than hormonal and physiological differences. 'We want to explain everything away by chemistry but it is really to do with the way society expects us to behave. There is not a link between levels of testosterone and accidents, murders and suicides. Men are encouraged to be laddish. They will discuss things about themselves which are not very deep. We would like to say the reason we have a problem is between our legs but in fact it is between our ears.'

Certainly when it comes to sex, there may well be a very 'between the ears' reason for men and women having different experiences and expectations. There may even be a physiological reason for men wanting 'a shag' and for women wanting to 'make love'. A study in *The Lancet* revealed that the brain area responsible for orgasms is different in men and women. In women it occurs in the right temporal lobe – one of the most advanced parts of the brain in evolutionary terms – while in men, the baser, more primitive hypothalamus has the pleasure.

Add all these physical reasons to some of the social factors – fathers preferring a night down the boozer to a session of *The Wind in the Willows* with their sons, or a man's fear of expressing his inner feelings and his inability to seek help – and it is little wonder that boys and men are falling

behind. It is a double-whammy, where men have allowed both the physical and social factors to conspire against them.

While the physiological gender differences are predetermined, Banks and others at the forefront of research into men's health, believe that there is no reason why society cannot work to overcome some of the pressures which drive men to self-destruction.

'Both the sexes have equal amounts of stress but while women will talk to their peers or doctors a man would rather bottle everything up. When it comes out it does so in a most dramatic way,' claims Banks.

'Men need to be encouraged to look after their bodies and health and we need to explore what makes a man a man. If we don't men will become more and more marginalised. This process needs to take place through media, education, industry and health.'

'It is wrong to say that women are outshining men in every area. We (men) are very good at killing ourselves, killing other people – especially women – having more accidents, getting more sports injuries and we excel at not seeing our doctors,' says Banks.

Ironically, despite the great strides made by women, it is still men who are at the forefront of media, health and industry – the areas where influence can be brought to bear. But do men have the will to help themselves?

• The above article appeared in *Focus* magazine.

© J.Carlowe, 1st April 1998

How women are faring in the US

Information from the quarterly update produced by Opportunity 2000

American women are twice as likely to reach the top of major companies as their British counterparts. But women in the US still hold only 10.6% of board positions in Fortune 500 companies, accounting for just 643 of a total of 6,081 board seats.

Dr Mary Mattis, head of research at Catalyst, a nonprofit research and advisory organisation working to advance women in business and the professions, expressed concern that although women have made considerable progress in US companies in recent years, the upward trend may be slowing. 'Some CEOs I have spoken to also believe the trend has topped out,' she said.

According to Ms Mattis' research, chief executives and female executives differ widely on the barriers to women's advancement. Over 80% of chief executives believe the main barrier to women's progress is that women lack significant general management experience. Only 46% of women, however, agree with this. For women it is stereotyped attitudes about their ambitions and abilities, their exclusion from male networks and inhospitable corporate cultures which are to blame.

Chief executives are also much more optimistic about the prospects for women's progress than their senior female managers. While nearly half of chief executives think that opportunities for women to advance to senior ranks have greatly improved over the last five years, only 23% of female executives agree.

Catalyst's research has also highlighted the strategies which effect change for women. According to Dr Mattis, good employers of women:
- demonstrate top level commitment to the need for change
- identify and track high potential women early on
- ensure these women get good all-round management experience by rotating them across functions

Over 80% of chief executives believe the main barrier to women's progress is that women lack significant general management experience

- create a comprehensive and sustained initiative in which the behaviour of managers is changed by linking equal opportunities goals to pay and bonuses
- take more risks with women and give them visible assignments
- provide mentoring and networking systems
- articulate a commitment to balance work/life responsibilities and remove barriers to flexibility.

© *Opportunity 2000*
Winter, 1997

Women and economic participation

Despite considerable progress in improving women's capabilities, women's participation in economic decision-making remains very limited. In developing countries, women still constitute less than a seventh of administrators and managers. Increased equity in decision-making is not only a matter of social justice, it is an essential requirement for the acceleration and effectiveness of development, as women are able to contribute their abilities. Studies also show that women's control of economic resources impacts directly on family health and nutrition.

- Women's recognised labour force participation has risen by only four percentage points in 20 years – from 36% in 1970 to 40% in 1990. Compare that with a two-thirds increase in female adult literacy and school enrollment.
- In developing countries, more than three-quarters of men's work is in paid activities, compared with only one-third of women's work. As a result, men receive the lion's share of income and recognition for their economic contribution – while most of women's work remains unpaid, unrecognised and undervalued.
- The failure to value women's work reduces women to virtual non-entities in most economic transactions – such as property ownership or offering collateral for bank loans.
- If women's unpaid work were properly valued, it is quite possible that women would emerge in most societies as the major breadwinners – or at least equal breadwinners – since they put in longer hours of work than men.
- Of the 1.3 billion people living in poverty world-wide, 70% are women.

© *Gender Action / USAID Office of Women in Development*

Women directors

The key findings from the executive summary of 'Women on the Boards of Britain's Top 200 Companies in 1997', produced by Opportunity 2000

Key findings

- The situation for women directors is better than the situation four years ago at the time of an earlier Ashridge survey. The number of women directors in the *Times* Top 200 British Companies has almost doubled since 1993.
- There are 109 board appointments held by 97 women – the first time the total number of appointments has moved into three figures.
- The absolute number of women remains a small minority – of the 2,000 plus director appointments women hold less than 5%.
- Women directors are more likely to be found among certain industry sectors – banks, building societies and retailing. The majority of banks, building societies and stores, for example, in the *Times* Top 200 have appointed women. The opposite is true for engineering and investment trusts.
- Most of the women directors identified in this survey are as likely to have gained their experience in the public arena as in commerce. A legal or financial

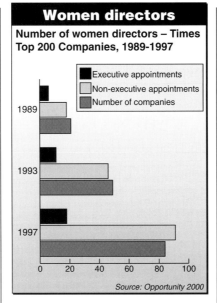

Women directors

Number of women directors – Times Top 200 Companies, 1989-1997

- ■ Executive appointments
- ☐ Non-executive appointments
- ▨ Number of companies

Source: Opportunity 2000

background is a strong theme but there are now more women with a media or customer-related background.

- Companies among the *Times* Top 200 are more likely to appoint a woman director than in the past and overall the number of women is increasing.
- Companies with women directors tend to be members of Opportunity 2000. Notable examples are J Sainsbury and Littlewoods,

both of whom were founding members of the Leadership Team.

- Women remain much more likely to hold non-executive, as opposed to executive directorships. The executive role is more senior and usually within the company. The non-executive role is generally held by an 'outsider', someone who is invited on to the board and holds the post for a limited term of office.
- The overwhelming majority of women in the survey (81%) remain the only women at board level. Encouragingly there is a significant increase in companies that have more than one woman director. A few have more than two women: such as the Co-operative Wholesale Society, with five women; and Marks & Spencer and Manchester Airport, each with three.

• The above is an extract from the executive summary of *Women on the Boards of Britain's Top 200 Companies in 1997*, produced by Opportunity 2000. See page 41 for address details.

© Opportunity 2000

Women still lag behind in pay and job stakes

By A. J. McIlroy and Charles Laurence

Men still lead the field when it comes to earnings and job status, even though women make up 51 per cent of the paid workforce, the Equal Opportunities Commission reported yesterday.

Women make up only 33 per cent of managers and administrators, six per cent of police sergeants and 15 per cent of legal partners.

Only one in 10 of the judiciary is a woman, while women comprise only 18 per cent of MPs and 31 per cent of public appointments.

Working full time, they continue to earn only 80 per cent of men's average hourly wage, which means that although the pay gap has narrowed, it has done so by only seven per cent in the past 20 years.

And even in retirement the differential is maintained, according to the commission's research. The average personal income of women aged 65-plus is only 58 per cent of the average for men in the same age group – a gender gap of 42 per cent.

The commission's report – *Facts About Women and Men 1997* – includes for the first time a grouping of 'equality indicators' compiled from its annual statistics to help to chart progress towards equality between the sexes.

These show that 51 per cent of unemployed women are in occupational groups in which at least 60 per cent of workers are women, the majority of whom are in secretarial, clerical, sales or similar work.

On the other hand, 65 per cent of employed men are in groups in which at least 60 per cent of workers are men, many of them managers or in professional occupations.

The commission reports that 67 per cent of the country's women and 77 per cent of men of working age have jobs. However, 45 per cent of women employees work part time, compared to eight per cent of men.

The commission reports that this is hardly surprising since its research shows that only one child in nine under the age of eight has a place in a nursery, with a registered childminder or in an out-of-school scheme. 'Some mothers have to find time to be at home to look after their children,' a spokesman said.

On average, a woman working full time earns slightly less than 75 per cent of an equivalent male colleague. This is down from 77 per cent in 1993

Kamlesh Bahl, the commission's chairman, said: 'These figures show that women are becoming more visible, but that there is no cause for complacency about their progress towards equality.'

She added: 'We will update the equality indicators annually to determine exactly what the facts are and to measure how far Britain is down the road towards genuine equality of opportunity.'

The income gap between the sexes has widened again in America, halting a 20-year trend in which working women had been catching up and, in some cases, overtaking men's earning levels.

New government figures show that on average, a woman working full time earns slightly less than 75 per cent of an equivalent male colleague. This is down from 77 per cent in 1993, the last time such a calculation was made.

It is unclear whether the reversal is a temporary stumble on the path to wage equality, or whether it reflects significant underlying changes in the job market and the nation's social structure.

Explanations have so far ranged from the 'workfare' welfare rules driving a new pool of lowest-wage female labour on to the market, distorting the average earnings figures, to the continuing dominance of women in childcare roles.

The Labour Bureau's figures shows that between 1979 and 1993, women's earning made steady progress from 62 per cent of men's to 77 per cent.

By 1993, young women in the lowest grades of work, often either black American or Hispanic, were making 101.6 per cent of their male colleagues' wages.

Claudia Goldin, an economist at Harvard University, told the *New York Times* yesterday that the figures pointed to a 'new equilibrium' in which women had been once more held at a disadvantage.

Army makes it easier for women to enlist

New 'gender-neutral' tests will remove sexual discrimination.
By Rachel Sylvester, Political Correspondent

The Army is to change the way it tests potential recruits, to give women a better chance of succeeding as part of a drive to remove sex discrimination from the Forces.

For the first time next week, men and women who want to join the Army will be put through an identical selection procedure, which will emphasise potential for a particular job rather than physical strength.

The Ministry of Defence has drawn up the new 'gender-neutral' tests, in consultation with the Equal Opportunities Commission, to boost the recruitment of women to the Army.

Simple tests of physical strength have been rejected because ministers and Army chiefs believe that they discriminate against women.

Instead, male and female applicants will face exactly the same challenges but the tests will depend on the type of work they want to do.

'Every job has a physical standard required and the new tests will be based on that,' an MoD source said. 'It does not matter if you are a man or a woman.'

The new procedure will be implemented for the first time from next Wednesday.

George Robertson, the Defence Secretary, and Gen. Sir Robin Wheeler, Chief of the Defence Staff, have pushed through the new procedure to open up the Armed Forces to a broader cross-section of the population.

Simple tests of physical strength have been rejected because ministers and Army chiefs believe that they discriminate against women

---

They have agreed to increase the proportion of jobs which can go to women from 47 per cent to 70 per cent from April 1. The Government is still reviewing the extent to which women should be sent to the front line. Ministry of Defence sources said the new tests did not amount to a 'levelling down' of fitness levels required from new recruits.

The Army has already been accused of softening its training because new recruits from the young 'couch potato' generation were not strong enough to cope with the physical demands of the traditional system. Ministers also deny that they are bowing to 'political correctness' by equalising tests despite physical differences between men and women.

'This is simply gender neutral,' an MoD source said. 'If women have to perform the same role as men, then they should be put through the same test.

'If the male or female applicant cannot do that, then they should not be accepted.'

New tests have been drawn up following two years of intensive physiological research to find the best way of identifying potential in applicants.

Ministers are determined to increase the number of women in the Army as a way of countering the shortfall of about 4,500 in troops.

In September, the last time for which figures are available, women represented only 6.3 per cent of the Army. There were 1,102 female officers and 5,746 other ranks.

The Government also wants to increase the number of recruits from ethnic minorities.

The gender divide

What makes girls and boys see things differently? Donald MacLeod on a revealing new survey

Girl: *'The kitchen is very big, it has lots of space for the things you need.'*

Boy: *'You can fit three cars in the garage.'*

Boys will be boys – but is it in their chromosomes that they are destined to fall behind girls at GCSE? Parents and teachers are often extremely concerned not to pigeon-hole children into stereotyped girl/boy roles and yet the differences surface in playgroup and widen through school. Why? And what should schools and parents do about it?

The clue lies in the choices children make from the earliest ages, according to a fascinating study by Patricia Murphy, of the Open University, and Jannette Elwood, of London University's Institute of Education. It is not what girls and boys can or cannot do but what they choose to do from playgroup onwards that matters.

Playgroup

Boys make straight for the construction toys or the bikes while the girls are playing in the home corner, doing a drawing or talking to an adult. Children have already developed clear ideas of what boys do and girls

do. 'Boys are racing all around the garden being somebody else or being the leader.' 'Girls – you find them sitting in a corner playing their quiet games,' were observations from playgroup staff. Boys tend to be Batman or at least a fireman while girls opt to be 'grand ladies' – so each are practising different types of talk, a mother-child discussion as opposed to arresting a baddie, for instance.

Boys made vehicles or guns, using moveable parts, while girls made simple houses to use in a social game

---

A study of pre-school children doing jigsaw puzzles found girls more often said 'I can't do this' or 'Where does this piece go?' There was no difference in their ability to solve the puzzles but when adults were shown videos of the children they judged the girls less confident and the boys' performance better. When

told the girls had done just as well, the adults said it was luck. Girls are likely to be influenced by this sort of feedback even if it is subtle rather than overt disapproval of them doing certain tasks.

Boys are expected to be interested in mechanical things and nursery and playgroup staff opt for books about tractors and dumpers to settle them down to listen to a book. Girls are more interested in drawing and more forward when it comes to using pencils and scissors, according to staff.

Reception

Boys arrive with an interest in information books and are likely to find reading schemes, based largely on stories about people, harder to get into, suggest Murphy and Elwood. They may also be at a disadvantage in learning to write because they are less good with pencils. 'The implication of this is that boys entering school are potentially more vulnerable than girls to becoming disaffected.'

Even when boys and girls are following the same activity like playing with Lego they are doing it

differently. Boys made vehicles or guns, using moveable parts, while girls made simple houses to use in a social game.

School

The stage is set for boys and girls to develop different styles of writing, influenced by the books they read. They are more likely to tackle tasks with confidence if they believe it is in their 'territory' and to see different aspects of what they observe as significant. Asked, for instance, to design a boat to go round the world, the girls include a kitchen and the boys a cannon. Writing an estate agent's blurb, one girl said: 'The kitchen is very big, it has lots of space for the things you need,' while a boy said: 'In the bathroom you could watch tele for the rest of our life with your free satilite (sic). And you can fit three cars in the garage.'

They describe the frustration of one girl working with a boy on a science task to test the time taken for sugar to dissolve in a cup of tea at different temperatures. The boy set up a range of temperatures starting with cold. 'Nobody drinks cold tea,' she protested. The teacher overruled the girl's objections and thought she was being difficult. The girl found the task pointless and alienating.

GCSE, A level

Girls' conformity at school is valued and encouraged but tends to make teachers underestimate their abilities. 'Ebullient, aggressive, risk-taking behaviour is often interpreted as an indicator of high ability,' comment Murphy and Elwood.

Good narrative and descriptive writing serves girls well at GCSE English where there is a 17 per cent lead over boys in A to C grades. The lead disappears in science where a different style of writing is favoured.

At A levels and at degree level more opinionated writing is preferred (although this may not be spelled out to students) and boys outperform girls at English and history.

'Teachers think they are giving them the same experience but what the children take away from it is different,' said Patricia Murphy.

Science vs poetry: two views of a demoiselle fly

Typical boy's response:
The demoiselle fly in general has a short thorax long abdomen and bulbous compound eyes.

Type A has all the aforementioned qualities but differs from type B in the following ways:
1. It has six long black legs with long hairs on top and lower parts of its legs.
Type B only has four legs and has hair's on the bottom of its forelegs and top of its hindlegs only.
2. Type A has opaque wings which are short and wide. Type B has transparent wings which are notably longer and thinner than type A's.
3. Type A has its abdomen segmented into fairly small parts, the end section tapering to a point. Type B has its abdomen made up of fairly small parts the end part tapering downwards to make it triangular.

Typical girl's response:
It is one of those lazy hot days in summer when everything is warm and very quiet. The trees surrounding the lake at the bottom of the hill are swaying silently and the ripples on the lake give the impression of peace and tranquillity. At the end of the lake are reeds and lilies. Flies buzz dozily among the tall grasses, looking for good (sic). Bees laze among the pollen filled lilies, drinking their sweet nectar and the demoiselle flies perch motionless on the tall green fronds of the reeds. There are two in particular, one male, one female, that catch my eye as I lie against the sturdy trunk of an ancient oak. They are the most beautiful creatures I have ever seen, but they are both different.

One has lacy wings, so clear I can see the water's edge through them. Its colouring is of brilliant pinks and blues, and it stands out amongst the yellow buttercups that surround it, its abdomen is long, like a finger, and incredibly thin.

It looks so fragile, as though any sudden movement may snap it, like a twig. Its lacy wings stretch back, almost to the full length of the abdomen, like delicate fans, cooling its body. Its head is small but bold. It is completely blue with piercing black eyes on either side of its head. The legs of this magnificent creature are long and black, with what look like hairs of the finest thread, placed at even spaces down each side. The thorax, the part next to its head, is large. It is not as slender as the abdomen, but it is very sleek, with patches of blue and black reflecting the brilliant sunlight.

As I watch, its head rotates and then suddenly it has disappeared hovering over the lake.

The other demoiselle fly still remains. This is not such a beautiful creature as the first, but it has striking markings. The wings are a dull brown in colour. They are much wider and not as long.

Girls outclassing boys

Survey reveals huge gender gap in almost all subjects. By John Carvel, Educational Editor

Teachers called last night for a government inquiry into the chronic underperformance of boys in almost all subjects and at all stages of compulsory education.

Doug McAvoy, general secretary of the National Union of Teachers, said he was alarmed at the size of the gender gap revealed in the first official analysis of the performance of 14-year-olds across the national curriculum.

Figures published yesterday by Estelle Morris, the school standards minister, showed about two-thirds of girls – but only half of boys – reached the expected level in history, geography, design and technology, modern foreign languages and music.

The girls also beat the boys by a wide margin in art and information technology – a subject in which boys were previously thought to excel.

In September the Government published results of national tests of 14-year-olds in the three core subjects of English, maths and science. They showed that girls outperformed boys in English, but did no better in maths and slightly worse in science.

In yesterday's analysis of other subjects, the only area of superior male achievements at the age of 14 was in physical education, in which 72 per cent of boys and 70 per cent of girls reached the expected standard.

The results showed teachers' assessment of the level reached by pupils at the end of Key Stage 3 of the national curriculum. There are no formal tests of performance in the non-core subjects at this age, and Ms Morris said her decision to publish the data was 'a reflection of the confidence we place in teachers' professional judgments'.

Mr McAvoy said the boys' low percentage scores were worrying. 'We are calling on the Government to commission urgent research to discover the social and educational causes.'

Pam Simmons, an authority on school effectiveness at the Institute of Education, London University, said there had long been evidence that girls outperformed boys at primary school, particularly in reading and verbal reasoning. In the 1960s and 1970s mixed grammar schools often set a lower admission standard for boys to ensure a gender balance.

At GCSE, 48 per cent of girls achieved at least five good passes at grade C or above, compared with 39 per cent of boys

---

Until recently boys tended to overtake girls at secondary school, with better marks at GCSE and A level. 'It is unlikely that girls' ability changed, but their expectations were raised and the introduction of the national curriculum helped equal opportunities. They are now more likely to be entered for exams at 15,' Ms Simmons said.

'There is no hard evidence that the performance of boys has declined, but we have to question whether many of them have become demotivated. The white working-class culture for boys is anti-education.'

At GCSE, 48 per cent of girls achieved at least five good passes at grade C or above, compared with 39 per cent of boys. A study this year found that schools failed by the Office for Standards in Education were more likely to have a predominance of boys on the roll. No all-girl school has been failed.

Next week the Qualifications and Curriculum Authority, which advises the Government on exams, will send out a teaching pack on how teachers can improve the performance of boys between seven and 16.

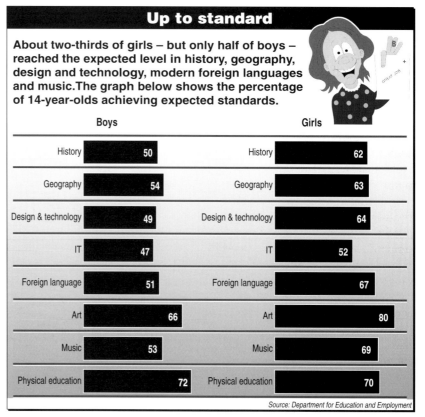

Up to standard

About two-thirds of girls – but only half of boys – reached the expected level in history, geography, design and technology, modern foreign languages and music. The graph below shows the percentage of 14-year-olds achieving expected standards.

Boys		Girls	
History	50	History	62
Geography	54	Geography	63
Design & technology	49	Design & technology	64
IT	47	IT	52
Foreign language	51	Foreign language	67
Art	66	Art	80
Music	53	Music	69
Physical education	72	Physical education	70

Source: Department for Education and Employment

Non-fiction tempts boys to catch up with the girls

Boys should be given fewer story books and more fact-based material if they are to catch up with girls at reading, schools are to be told. The move was revealed as the Government announced a range of measures to redress the balance. Fran Abrams, Political Correspondent, says it could prove controversial

Everyone agrees that something has to be done to stop boys from falling further behind girls at school. But not everyone agrees on how to do it.

Figures in the new guidance being sent to all schools this month provide stark reading, and they show that the gender gap appears early. At seven, 21 per cent of girls reach National Curriculum level three in English, compared with just 14 per cent of boys. At 11, level four is reached by 69 per cent of girls and 57 per cent of boys, and at 14, level five is reached by 66 per cent of girls and 47 per cent of boys.

Now the Qualifications and Curriculum Authority is suggesting that boys might do better if the non-fiction books they read at home were used more in school.

But some English experts are worried that the approach will simply reinforce stereotypes. They agree with the Government's advisers that boys should be helped to catch up through clear goals and more structured lessons. But Ann Barnes, general secretary of the National Association for the Teaching of English, said restricting boys' chances to read stories would be wrong.

'If that's what we are going towards that is a really serious mistake, and a seriously narrow menu to put in front of them. It is important to get them to read whatever they want to read, but I think it would be a great mistake to just feed boys factual things,' she said.

The QCA's guidance says inspectors have found that few teachers monitor the differences in boys' and girls' reading patterns effectively. They also found poetry was less popular with boys, who often preferred active pursuits to the more 'sedentary' reading and writing.

However, boys at secondary school enjoyed performing, and were often articulate and adventurous in oral sessions. They often read extensively and regularly about their interests and hobbies, but felt that their schools took little account of this.

> ### Some English experts are worried that the approach will simply reinforce stereotypes

'They had to be cautious about admitting their pleasure in reading because of negative peer group pressure. They often had to make links with girls or rely on adults for recommendations and for oppor-tunities to share their interest in books,' one case study says.

Boys' stories often failed to meet the criteria for high grades at GCSE because although they were action-packed and imaginative they were also poorly plotted and weak on characterisation. Girls, on the other hand, placed more emphasis on emotions and characters.

A spokeswoman from the QCA said the guidance aimed to provide practical tips on how to help boys.

'Can Do Better takes the issue of boys' underachievement one step further beyond the stereotypes, for example by looking at how aspects of school life and teaching arrange-ments impact on boys' work and attitudes to English,' she said.

The new guidance will follow a speech yesterday in Manchester by Stephen Byers, the schools minister, who blamed 'laddish anti-learning culture' for boys' poor performance.

© *The Independent*
January, 1998

Problems that arise when boys will be lads

By Vivek Chaudhary, Education Correspondent

New laddism – or just an old-fashioned problem of boys behaving badly? As the Government and educationists contemplate the latest figures suggesting that under-achieving by boys at school is more serious than ever before, many believe that the root of the problem lies as much within the education system as in the changing nature of society.

Stephen Byers, the School Standards Minister, yesterday announced the need for more male teachers to provide boys with role models and combat the 'laddish' attitude that has led to boys trailing behind girls at every stage of education.

Just over a decade ago it was girls who were under-achieving, with fewer going to university or into the professions despite the fact that they did better in exams.

Greg Brookes, of the National Foundation for Educational Research, who has examined gender differences in education, said: 'Girls have always done better but that gap is more marked now than ever before.

'Boys tended to catch up in secondary schools, but increasingly over the last 10 to 15 years the girls have been staying ahead and the boys have not been catching up at the later stages.'

According to latest figures released by the Government, girls now outperform boys at getting five good GCSE grades. They also outperform boys in national curriculum tests at seven, 11 and 14.

For many, however, it is a combination of factors, ranging from the changing nature of the workplace to the revised education system, that has led to the decline of boys' performance at school.

Dr Brookes said: 'We found that by the time many boys got to secondary school, they had limited prospects and ambitions.

'This is probably due to the closing down of unskilled manual work and the increase in jobs in the service industry, which favours women.'

'In Switzerland and the Scandinavian countries, there are less gender differences in education. The whole class is taken forward'

Dr Brookes also agreed with the Government on the need for more male teachers, particularly in primary schools. 'A lot of boys only see their mothers reading at home and female teachers reading in the classroom. Reading is seen as a female pursuit, and not a masculine one.'

Researchers have found that the GCSE examination system, which relies heavily on course work, also favours girls rather than boys.

Alan Smithers, director of the Centre for Education and Employment Research, based at Brunel University, said: 'Girls are more conscientious and better able to prepare for course work. Boys have been found to be better at exams and multiple choice questions.'

Prof. Smithers believes that the key to improving the educational performance of boys lies in the nursery. 'There is too much emphasis on getting children to read at an early age. Girls are able to deal with it better.

'In Switzerland and the Scandinavian countries, there are fewer gender differences in education. The whole class is taken forward. There is less emphasis on success or failure.' He added: 'The emphasis in Britain is on individual differences.'

Almost 15 years ago, the then Education Secretary, Sir Keith Joseph, called for the education system to be more responsive to the needs of girls, who he said were not reaching their potential. Mr Smithers said: 'Before, girls could not quite see the incentives of working hard to get an education. They now see the relationship between education and work. We need to be able to do the same for boys.'

Pupil: *'Not all girls are clever. Most of the girls smoke and lots of them bunk off as well. Quite a lot do it but girls are the worst'*

There are, says Daniel Farrell, three categories of pupils who might incur the wrath of their classmates at the school he attends in north London; weirdos, those who sound posh, and swots.

'If you're too clever then a lot of people don't like you because they think you're teacher's pet. Other kids will start cussing you in the playground but it's not just those who are too clever who might get stick. It's anyone who stands out, someone who is fat or a geek,' said Daniel, aged 13.

A pupil at the St Thomas More school, a mixed comprehensive in Wood Green, north London, Daniel admits that being too clever can be a bit of a hindrance rather than an advantage at his school.

He said: 'I get a bit of stick myself because I really like English. Sometimes I don't bother answering or asking questions in class because I worry that my friends will take the mickey out of me for being teacher's pet.'

An intelligent boy who enjoys academic lessons as well as sport, Daniel claims that peer group pressure had led some of his friends to ignore their studies and misbehave in school.

'A lot of kids in school smoke because of their friends and other kids I know don't bother with lessons because of their mates. Some children misbehave because they don't want to be seen to be too clever.'

Daniel would like to go to university.

He has not decided what job he wants, but is convinced that a good education is important.

'Education is a bit channelled towards just doing exams and I would like to learn a bit more.'

Daniel is dismissive of claims by education specialists who claim that girls do much better at school than boys.

'Not all girls are clever. In my school most of the girls smoke and lots of them bunk off as well. Quite a lot of the pupils do it but the girls are the worst.'

'If you're too clever then a lot of people don't like you because they think you're teacher's pet. Other kids will start cussing you in the playground'

Teacher: *'A lot of alienation is down to peer pressure on boys not to be seen as swots. It has a tremendous impact'*

For almost 20 years of his teaching career John Illingworth was a rare commodity: a male teacher working in a junior school.

Now headmaster at the Brookhill Leys junior school in Eastwood, near Nottingham, Mr Illingworth claims that while he has witnessed increased alienation among young boys towards education there has been no increase in the number of male teachers working in primary and junior schools.

There are only two male teachers among the staff of nine, but, claims Mr Illingworth, aged 46, his main concern is the reluctance of boys in his school to study.

'A lot of alienation is down to peer pressure on boys not to be seen as swots. It has a tremendous impact.

A worrying subculture has emerged that is almost anti-education.'

Mr Illingworth, who began teaching in 1973, claims that the attitude of boys towards studying and wanting to succeed via education has deteriorated over the years.

He maintains that the reasons for underachievement among boys lie outside school, within society, not simply in the lack of male teachers. While almost 88 per cent of primary and junior school teachers are women the majority of head-masters for such schools are men.

'There have always been more women teachers than men in primary schools, even when boys were doing much better. The problem facing boys is much wider and more complex than that.'

The school is in a former mining town suffering from high unemployment, and Mr Illingworth claims that this, plus a lack of positive role models for boys, are crucial factors which go some way to explain why boys under-achieve. The other reason was that lessons were just too boring for restless boys.

'There is a total lack of stimulation in the national curriculum. Class sizes are also much bigger, which makes discipline harder to enforce, and we are working in a deprived area.' *© The Guardian January, 1998*

Examination achievements of pupils in school

Girls do markedly better than boys at GCSE – a full 10 per cent more girls than boys obtained at least five grades A to C in 1995/96. However, in terms of two or more A levels there is a narrower gap with 23 per cent of girls obtaining these qualifications compared with 20 per cent of boys.

	2 or more GCE A levels[1]		5 or more GCSEs grades A-C[2]		No graded GCSEs[2]	
	Males	Females	Males	Females	Males	Females
England	19	21	40	49	9	7
Wales	18	23	37	47	12	9
Scotland	28	35	47	60	5	3
Northern Ireland	26	37	45	59	7	3
United Kingdom	20	23	41	51	9	6

[1] Pupils aged 17 to 19 at the end of the school year in England, Wales and Northern Ireland as a percentage of the 18-year-old population. For Scotland the figures relate to pupils in years S5/S6 gaining three or more SCE Higher passes as a percentage of the 17-year-old population.
[2] Pupils aged 16 at the end of the school year as a percentage of the 15-year-old population at start of school year. Scotland pupils are in year S4.

Source: Department for Education and Employment; Welsh Office; The Scottish Office Education and Industry Department; Department of Education Northern Ireland

Will the boys who can't read still end up as the men on top?

By Ann Treneman

Boys!' said one mother the other day as we watched several toddler-sized males behaving badly. 'They are so different from girls. I never believed it until I had mine.' One lad then started to decapitate a lamp. 'Oh, he's got so much energy,' said his mum as furniture started to fly.

I report this conversation not because it is rare but because it is so common. Every parent has had it at least a thousand times and so I hardly think it is a secret that boys behave badly and have since forever. Every mum and dad knows this. Every sister with a brother knows this. Every tomboy who tried to get away with it herself knows it. Every teacher knows it. Even that guy called Anon who came up with the puppydog tail line knew it. And now, it seems, the Government does too.

Yesterday the papers were full of the 'news' that girls are better than boys at school and the 'laddish anti-learning culture' is to blame. Official figures released today show girls outperforming boys at GCSE level in all but one local authority. The Government has declared this to be a crisis and is acting accordingly. Schools minister Stephen Byers – a member of the Prime Minister's Social Exclusion Unit – is to announce a national strategy to deal with the gender gap. 'From this point of view the most worrying thing is this men behaving badly type of culture where learning is out and mucking about is in,' said a spokesman for the education department yesterday. The Government is to make disaffected boys a central issue of its European presidency.

The first reaction to this has to be whether things haven't got a little bit out of perspective here. After all, the statistical under-achievement of boys in schools is nothing compared with the statistical over-achievement of men in life. To look at the figures,

it would seem that the boy who cannot read as well as the girl next door at age seven will make up for that rather nicely over the coming decade or two. By the time they get to university, for instance, he will start to draw even and eventually pull ahead. At work he will make about 20 per cent more money than she does and have an astronomically better chance of getting a bit of real power in terms of a seat on the board.

> *The papers were full of the 'news' that girls are better than boys at school and the 'laddish anti-learning culture' is to blame*

His personal life also has more choice and less drudgery. The average man spends three minutes a day doing laundry, according to the National Statistics Office. Now that's a figure that tells a story.

It's not only New Lad who is mucking about. Witness West-

minster, the ultimate place for men behaving badly. This has not gone unnoticed by the 120 women MPs, many of whom are newcomers to this particular playground and do not like what they have found. In *Westminster Women*, a new ITV series which began yesterday, the Labour MP for Reading East, Jane Griffiths, talked about two Conservative MPs who put their hands out in front of their breasts 'as if weighing melons' when female members speak. A survey for the series by the gender equality group Fawcett showed that 63 per cent of female MPs think it is harder to be a woman than a man in Parliament. The reasons? 'Yob culture', 'male public school attitudes', 'silly rules and secret conventions . . . managed by men, for men'.

Labour men behave badly too, of course, and it is rather interesting that the Government is so concerned about boys in general behaving badly when there are probably some rather needy disciplinary cases closer to hand. But there are deeper currents at work here in both Parliament and the primary school and both have far-reaching implications. After all, the figures do not tell the whole story because today's boy of 10 and his father come from generations that are getting more different by the day. The world of work, particularly for the working class, is changing rapidly. Manufacturing jobs are in decline. Information technology and leisure are the new growth areas. There are fewer 'jobs for life' and more part-time and short-term contract work. Women are in the workplace to stay. Eventually – they say – the glass ceiling will only be a memory. These changes, some call it a revolution, have important consequences and it will mean that the lad of 10 may not be able to get away with behaving badly when he is his father's age.

My Byers today will call on local education authorities to draw up plans to tackle the problem. One of the areas is likely to be whether boys have enough role models in primary school. The reasons for this are simple: low pay. There is talk of a drive to increase the pay of primary teachers to attract more men into the junior schools (women can only welcome such an idea though it's a pretty back-handed compliment). Then there is also the area of voluntary classroom assistants. At the moment it is much more likely to be a mum who offers her time to help. 'It has been shown that boys see reading as something that is feminine,' said an education department spokesman yesterday. 'It may be that schools will try to get more fathers in to read.'

The idea of getting more fathers in to show little Johnny that reading can be masculine is almost as wonderful as the idea of getting more women in Parliament to show that governing can be feminine. Perhaps Girl Power – that feel-good factor for every female under eight – may not so much trickle down as percolate up.

Certainly the new female MPs have the confidence to challenge the *status quo*. 'These women want to change the definition of what an MP actually is,' says Mary-Ann Stephenson of Fawcett. 'They don't want Parliament to stay the way it is. They want it to change.'

Can it happen? Will there be huge increases in the number of female MPs and male primary school teachers? Whatever lies ahead, the two are linked: the culture of playground and of Parliament have too much in common for it to be otherwise.

© *The Independent*
January, 1998

Confidence trick

While schoolgirls leave the boys standing, university finals see a dramatic reversal of fortune. Donald MacLeod reports

Women students become far more anxious about examinations than their male counterparts, and their less confident performance could mean missing out on first-class degrees, according to a study at Oxford University.

While ministers and teachers agonise about the failure of boys to keep up with the girls in the school classroom, Oxford and Cambridge are still trying to pinpoint the reasons why female students who excel at A level do so badly in their final exams compared to men. At both universities, more than 16 per cent of male candidates are awarded first-class degrees, compared to about 9 per cent of women. For women whose ambition is an academic career, failure to get a first is likely to prove an insurmountable barrier.

Theories to explain the relative decline of women's achievement at Oxbridge since the 1970s range from the laddish culture of the formerly all-male colleges to the introduction of comprehensive schooling, to the higher numbers of private school girls selected by admissions tutors.

Several academics have suggested that Oxbridge examiners tend to reward bold, assertive essays – the typically male style – rather than the painstaking and cautious work more often produced by female undergraduates.

Maryanne Martin, a psychology lecturer and fellow of St Edmund Hall, Oxford, tested 200 students to see how anxious they were about exams. Questionnaires also assessed their long- and short-term mood. They were selected as either close to their next exam (within a week) or relatively distant (at least six weeks away).

Both general, short-term anxiety and specific examination anxiety was higher in the group about to take their exams, but the study found significantly higher levels among women students. In fact, the men showed less exam anxiety close

---

Oxford and Cambridge are still trying to pinpoint the reasons why female students who excel at A level do so badly in their final exams compared to men

---

to an exam than the women showed six weeks before their papers.

In the latest issue of the *Oxford Review of Education*, Ms Martin suggests: 'It is possible that the greater anxiety and imagery concerning examinations and grading which were found among female students underlie a tendency for female students to exhibit an academic style in written or spoken work which is more cautious and less confident than that of male students.'

She argues it is time for academics to look at how they assess students. 'In particular, is the boldness with which an argument is presented an appropriate criterion to be used in evaluating a student's academic achievement?'

A consensus among academics that a cautious style should not be valued less highly than a confident one could reduce differences between male and female performance in degrees. But if a confident style was to be confirmed as the mark of a first, then students lacking confidence should be better supported, either by special help with essay writing or measures to try and reduce levels of anxiety, argues Ms Martin.

© *The Guardian*
January, 1998

WISE bus stops those misconceptions

Lee Rodwell reports on a scheme to persuade girls to take up engineering and science careers

It started with one bus. Now there are four and a trailer, travelling round the country to persuade schoolgirls they can be scientists and engineers. The WISE (Women Into Science & Engineering) bus initiative was launched by the Engineering Council in 1984. In a recent evaluation, 92 per cent of the year nine girls who came aboard to go through the programme said it had an impact, and 19 per cent said they now wanted to go into engineering.

But now that all children have to take science up to GCSE, are the buses still necessary? 'Definitely,' says Marie-Noelle Barton, WISE campaign manager.

'Increasingly girls seem to be able to take only biology at GCSE, or general sciences. That means they are not doing physics or chemistry. That in turn means they are closing the door at 16 on a range of career options, such as medicine and engineering.'

Besides, the buses offer girls a chance to get their hands on various technologies away from the boys. 'Often schools have the equipment,' says Marie-Noelle, 'but the boys always get there first. On a bus the girls can use it for an hour and a half at their own pace.

'It also helps them understand how engineering permeates every aspect of life. We have a scale model of a bus door, so they can see what happens when you press the button to open it. Another model is of disco lights – they can see the electronics which creates the effects they see on a Saturday night.

'And we normally have young women engineers on the bus so the girls can meet them and realise there is nothing odd about them. They are just ordinary women who shop in Sainsbury's and have families like

anyone else. It changes their idea that an engineer is a man in a greasy overall waving a spanner.'

The WISE buses have been a great success with secondary schools. Now there are plans to target younger children. Next year, the WISE campaign will launch a booklet for primary school teachers and parents and a poster which will go into all the UK's 24,000 primary schools. It will show young children how exciting engineering and technology is and how suitable a career it is for girls.

Marie-Noelle Barton is almost evangelical about getting the message across to girls. 'There is a great deal to be said for choosing engineering. Sponsorships are available for degree courses, which is important in these days of trying to pay off student loans.

'The prospects for becoming high earners and for working abroad are very real. You are at the forefront of technology and, above all, you are in a caring profession.

'Often schools have the equipment, but the boys always get there first. On a bus the girls can use it for an hour and a half at their own pace'

'People think of engineers as those who make cars, planes, trains, dams and bridges. In fact, engineering is about people. It's about getting people from A to B. It's about conserving the food we eat, producing the energy we need to heat our homes.

'I often ask girls to think about a tiny baby with a heart condition. Who is the life saver – the doctor who performs the surgery or the person who made the scanners and incubator?'

- Northampton engineering firm Express Lifts sends engineering apprentices into a local primary school to work with children and teachers on science-based projects. This year the task is to build an iron man.
- BP and the University of Sunderland run student tutoring schemes whereby undergraduates are sponsored to work in nursery, primary and secondary schools to help out on science projects.
- British Gas (Wales) visited schools to give year 10 girls a presentation about becoming service engineers. They showed a video of women service engineers at work and invited the girls to take part in a range of apprentice aptitude tests.
- Chartwell Land sponsors female students through a degree course to attract women into surveying. The sponsorship also includes work experience during university vacations.
- BT has a long-term partnership with the all-girls Sacred Heart High School in North London which ensures all girls are familiar with modern IT systems and equipment.

© The Independent December, 1996

ADDITIONAL RESOURCES

You might like to contact the following organisations for further information. Due to the increasing cost of postage, many organisations cannot respond to enquiries unless they receive a stamped, addressed envelope.

300 Group
PO Box 353
Uxbridge
Middlesex, UB10 0UN
Tel: 01895 812229
Fax: 01895 812229
Campaigns to bring more women into Parliament and to encourage more women to participate in decision-making in all areas of public life. Produces publications.

Business and Professional Women UK Ltd (BPW UK)
23 Ansdell Street
London, W8 5BN
Tel: 0171 938 1729
Fax: 0171 938 2037
Promotes a free and responsible society in which women take an active part in decision-making at all levels; encourages co-operation and fosters understanding among women throughout the world. Produces publications.

City Women's Network
PO Box 353
Uxbridge
Middlesex, UB10 0UN
Tel: 01895 272178
The UK's leading network for senior executive women. Promotes networking on business, professional and social levels. Produces publications.

Demos
9 Bridewell Place
London, EC4V 6AP
Tel: 0171 353 4479
Fax: 0171 353 4481
Demos is an independent think-tank committed to radical thinking on the long-term problems facing the UK and other advanced industrial societies. Their new book, *Tomorrow's Women*, (ISBN 1 898309 48 5, price £9:95) is a provocative report which is set to spark a national debate on the future of women's lives. Available from all good bookshops or direct from Demos

Equal Opportunities Commission
Overseas House
Quay Street
Manchester, M3 3HN
Tel: 0161 833 9244
Fax: 0161 835 1657
Works toward the elimination of unlawful sexual and marriage discrimination, to promote equality of opportunities between women and men generally and to keep the Sex Discrimination Act and Equal Pay Act under review.

European Commission Office (UK)
8 Storey's Gate
London, SW1P 3AT
Tel: 0171 973 1992
Fax: 0171 973 1900
The European Commission Office identifies three distinct functions: initiating proposals for legislation, guardian of the treaties, and the management and executor of Union policies and of international industry trade relationships.

Fawcett Society
5th Floor
45 Beech Street
London, EC2Y 8AD
Tel: 0171 628 4441
Fax: 0171 628 2865
To influence parliament and public opinion to accept equal status for women in the home and public life, and equal educational and job opportunities. Publish *Towards Equality*, a quarterly publication. To subscribe to *Towards Equality* and other publications send £25.00 to: Fawcett Society, Freepost FE 6903, London, EC2B 2JD.

Industrial Society
Robert Hyde House
48 Bryanston Square
London, W1H 7LN
Tel: 0171 262 2401
Fax: 0171 724 3354
Produces a range of booklets and

information packs on all sorts of work related issues including: working mothers, racial and sexual harassment, smoking and alcohol policies. Their library includes a wide range of press cuttings and employment statistics.

Low Pay Unit
27-29 Amwell Street
London, EC1R 1UN
Tel: 0171 713 7616
Fax: 0171 713 7581
Investigates low pay, poverty and related issues. Produces publications.

National Council of Women of Great Britain
36 Danbury Street
London, N1 8JU
Tel: 0171 354 2395
Fax: 0171 354 9214
Works towards the removal of discrimination against women. Produces publications.

Opportunity 2000
44 Baker Street
London, W1M 1DH
Tel: 0171 224 1600
Fax: 0171 486 1700
Opportunity 2000 is a business-led campaign with one clear objective – to increase the quality of women's employment opportunities in private and public sector organisations. Produces publications although these are aimed more towards businesses than students.

Womankind Worldwide
3 Albion Place
Galena Road
London, W6 0LT
Tel: 0181 563 8607/8
Supports and fund-raiser for women in developing countries, To work with them to overcome poverty, to educate them and train them to ensure better health and to give women greater control over their own lives.

INDEX

advertising, portrayal of men in 24, 26
age discrimination 18
armed forces
    and the sex discrimination laws 8, 14
Asian countries, women managers 9-10

benefits (employment), and equal pay 2
benefits (state), and indirect discrimination 1
boys
    and education 32-9
        achievements compared with girls 4, 25, 32-6
        national curriculum 34
        reading 35, 36, 39
brains, of men and women 26-7
business, women and 12-13, 25, 28, 29

car insurance, and gender pricing 20

deaths, gender differences in 22
developing countries, women's work in 28
directors, women 29
discrimination
    against men 21-4
    direct and indirect 1, 6, 18
    gender discrimination in pricing 20
    marriage 6-7
    race 18

earnings see pay
education 32-40
    discrimination against men in 23-4
    male teachers 23, 36, 37, 39
    national curriculum 34, 35, 36
    universities 39
    women and 11, 39
        science and engineering 40
employment
    best practice guidelines 19
    changing patterns of, and men 38
    and European Union law 1-3
    hours of work 17, 24
    occupations
        segregation by gender 10
        sex-stereotyped 8-9, 16, 30
    and the Sex Discrimination Acts 6-8
    victimisation 7
    see also women, and employment
engineering, women and careers in 40
English, gender differences in performance 34, 35
equal opportunities
    in education 32-40
    in the workplace 1-31
Equal Opportunities Commission (EOC) 4, 6-8, 13-14, 30
    and the armed forces 31
    Code of Practice on Equal Pay 17
Equal Pay Act (1970) 6
ethnic minorities, and the armed services 31
European countries
    earnings gap 19
    women managers 9
European Union (EU)
    Code on the Dignity of Men and Women at Work 19
    employment law 1-3, 18

examination results
    girls compared with boys 4, 25, 32, 33, 34, 35, 36, 37
    universities 39
fathers
    and children in schools 23-4
    losing contact with children 23, 24
Fawcett Society 16-17, 38, 39
feminine values 11-13
feminism 11-12, 13
flexible working patterns 12, 15, 17

genetics, and sex differences 26-7
girls
    and education 34-5
        achievements compared with boys 4, 25, 32-6
        national curriculum 34
glass ceiling 8, 12

hairdressers, and gender pricing 20
health, gender differences in 22, 25, 27

job classification systems 2
job-sharing 17

laddish culture
    in schools 35, 36, 37, 38
    in universities 39
libraries, and discrimination against men 22
life expectancy, by gender 25

management, women in 8-10, 11, 13, 28, 30
marriage
    benefits to men of 26
    discrimination 6-7
    divorce and gender 23
men
    attitudes to work 15, 16
    behaving badly 38
    and changing gender roles 12
    discrimination against 21-4
    as a proportion of occupational groups 4
MPs (Members of Parliament), women 38, 39

national curriculum, gender differences in performance 34, 35, 36
new age values, and women 12
newspapers, discrimination against men in 24

part-time workers
    by gender 4
    and indirect discrimination 1
    and training 5
    women 16, 17, 30
    and work of equal value 2
pay
    equal pay for equal work 1-2
    equal pay for work of equal value 2, 14, 16-17
    gender pay gap 4, 13, 16, 18, 19, 30
    of primary school teachers 39
    professional women 9
pensions, Occupational Pensions Schemes 8
physical education, boys compared with girls 34
politics, women and 13
pregnancy, and workplace discrimination 1, 8
pricing, gender discrimination in 20

primary schools
    engineering projects 40
    male teachers 23, 36, 37, 39
professional women
    hours of work 17
    pay 9
promotion, and equal treatment in the workplace 3, 13

science, women and careers in 40
Sex Discrimination Acts (1975 and 1986) 6-8, 20
sexual harassment 19
sport, women and 25

trade unions, and equal pay for work of equal value 2
training
    women and 5

unemployment
    and boys' underachievement at school 37
    and women 30
United Kingdom Men's Movement 21

vocational training
    discrimination in the workplace 5
    and equal treatment in the workplace 3

women
    and changing gender roles 12
    characteristics of tomorrow's women 11-13, 15-16,
        25-6
    and economic participation 28
    and employment 11-13, 16-17
        business 12-13, 25, 28, 29
        managers 8-10, 11, 13, 28, 30
        new Equal Treatment Act 13-14
        pay compared with men 4, 5
        and pregnancy 1, 8
        professional women 9, 17
        as a proportion of occupational groups 3, 4
        young women 15-16
        see also pay
    sporting achievements 25
    unemployed 30
    university students 39
workfare, and women's pay 30

young women
    and car insurance 20
    and employment 15-16

Independence Web News

Back | Forward | Home | Reload | Images | Open | Print | Find | Stop

Live Home Page | Search | Computer | Support | System

The Internet has been likened to shopping in a supermarket without aisles. The press of a button on a Web browser can bring up thousands of sites but working your way through them to find what you want can involve long and frustrating on-line searches. And unfortunately many sites contain inaccurate, misleading or heavily biased information. Our researchers have therefore undertaken an extensive analysis to bring you a selection of quality Web site addresses. If our readers feel that this new innovation in the series is useful, we plan to provide a more extensive Web site section in each new book in the *Issues* series.

★ ★ ★ ★ ★

Equal Opportunities Commission
www.eoc.org.uk
The Equal Opportunities Commission is the expert body on equality between women and men. Its site provides a comprehensive coverage of equal opportunity issues.

Equality between women and men
www.dhdirhr.coe.fr/Intro/eng/GENERAL/equality.htm
This web site is maintained by the Directorate of Human Rights of the Council of Europe to facilitate public access to information about the Human Rights Activities of the Council of Europe.

European Commission
http://citizens.eu.int/en/en/gf/eq/en/giindex.htm
This site provides a range of equal opportunity factsheets, outlining your rights in each of the 15 Member States. Included are names, addresses and phone numbers of relevant organisations and cover a wide range of topics; for example, how to protect yourself against unfair contract terms.

European Women's Lobby
www.womenlobby.org
The European Women's Lobby (EWL) is the largest co-ordinating body of national and European non-governmental women's organisation in the European Union.

The United Nations Division for the Advancement of Women (DAW)
www.un.org/womenwatch/daw
DAW advocates the improvement of the status of the women of the world and the achievement of their equality with men.

UK Men and Father's Rights
www.coeffic.demon.co.uk
Puts the case for men's rights claiming it is men rather than women who are the real victims of sexual discrimination. This site contain thought-provoking articles which are sure to stimulate debate.

ACKNOWLEDGEMENTS

The publisher is grateful for permission to reproduce the following material.

While every care has been taken to trace and acknowledge copyright, the publisher tenders its apology for any accidental infringement or where copyright has proved untraceable. The publisher would be pleased to come to a suitable arrangement in any such case with the rightful owner.

Chapter One: The Workplace

Citizens first, © Office for the Official Publications of the European Communities, *Women as a proportion of occupational groups in the European Union, 1995 %*, © European Commission, DGV (1997), *Equality indicators*, © European Opportunities Commission, *Women's earnings as a percentage of men's earnings: by industry*, © Social Trends, Office for National Statistics, Crown Copyright 1998, *Women at a disadvantage in the labour market*, © Policy Studies Institute, April 1998, *Equal Opportunities*, © Equal Opportunities Commission, *'Glass ceiling' separates women from top jobs*, © International Labour Office, *Administrative and managerial jobs*, © International Labour Office, *Tomorrow's women*, © Demos, *Wanted: a tough new law to promote women*, © The Independent, January 1998, *The future: focused, flexible and female*, © The Independent, November 1997, *Women and employment*, © Fawcett Society, *Key facts and guidance for managers*, © The Industrial Society, *Sex and shopping*, © The Independent, January 1998, *Militant men declare war on 'social evil of feminism'*, © The Independent, February 1997, *Discrimination against men*, © B. Robertson, Cambridge Men's Action Group, *Gene wars*, © J. Carlowe, 1st April 1998, *How women are faring in the US*, © Opportunity 2000, Winter 1997, *Women and economic participation*, © Gender Action / US AID Office of Women in Development, *Women directors*, © Opportunity 2000, *Women still lag behind in pay and job stakes*, © Telegraph Group Limited, London 1997, *Army makes it easier for women to enlist*, © Telegraph Group Limited, London 1998.

Chapter Two: Education

The gender divide, © The Guardian, June 1997, *Science vs poetry: two views of a demoiselle fly*, © The Guardian, June 1997, *Girls outclassing boys*, © The Guardian, November 1997, *Non-fiction tempts boys to catch up with the girls*, © The Independent, January 1998, *Problems that arise when boys will be lads*, © The Guardian, January 1998, *Examination achievements of pupils in school*, © Social Trends, Office for National Statistics, Crown Copyright 1998, *Will the boys who can't read end up as the men on top?*, © The Independent, January 1998, *Confidence trick*, © The Guardian, January 1998, *WISE bus stops those misconceptions*, © The Independent, December 1996.

Photographs and illustrations:

Pages 1, 7, 17, 18, 27, 32, 35: The Attic Publishing Co., pages 10, 12, 21, 22, 29, 31: Ken Pyne, page 36: Andrew Smith.

Thank you

Darin Jewell for assisting in the editorial research for this publication.

Craig Donnellan
Cambridge
September, 1998